HEART
—OVER—
HEIGHT

NATE ROBINSON
WITH JON FINKEL

Front Cover designed by: Chris Hobrecker
Edited by: Jared Evans

ISBN: 978-1-4834-1303-7 (sc)
ISBN: 978-1-4834-1302-0 (e)

Library of Congress Control Number: 2014909719

Image on the back cover: Stacy Barnett/Shutterstock.com

Lulu Publishing Services rev. date: 05/29/2014

DEDICATIONS

You might think it's tough to be 5'9" and playing in the NBA, but it's nothing compared to raising a bunch of kids and half a neighborhood by yourself. That's why this book is dedicated to one of the strongest people I know, my mother. I also dedicate this book to my brothers and sisters and family members who have believed in me and the pursuit of my dreams every step of the way, from middle school to Madison Square Garden. The people and the city of Seattle also deserve credit for helping me become who I am today. I also have to thank all of my fans from all of the cities I've played in—your love and support continue to make playing this amazing game of basketball every day a dream. And to my children: You are my legacy and my life, and I love you. I am truly blessed.

INTRODUCTION

27 points, 9 assists, 10 stitches.

I'll take that stat line any day of the week, especially in the playoffs. The points and assists came from never giving up. The stitches came from never giving in. I can still feel the scar in my mouth, but I'm used to scars. I have scars and scratches all over my face from when I was a little boy. Neighborhood kids called me Scarface and every other ugly name you could think of. But this new scar on my face is different. It didn't come from a playground fall or neighborhood scuffle or wrestling with my brother; this scar is from LeBron James' whole body grinding my face into the hardwood floor while we dove for a loose ball in Game 1 of the second round of the playoffs in 2013.

The play happened fast. The ball was skipping across the court and since I couldn't tell if it bounced off one of my teammates or not, I reacted and chased after it. LeBron did too, and when we were close enough we both dove for it—just two great players going at it, hustling, willing to sacrifice our bodies for our teammates in the name of winning. The thing is, my body is 5'9" and 185 pounds and LeBron's body is about 6'8", 270. No way I'm coming out of that unscathed.

As soon as I hit the ground, it felt like every ounce of his weight crashed onto my head. My first thought was that all of my teeth were knocked out. I've seen that happen before, where a guy comes down on another guy and the guy on the bottom loses his teeth. I felt for my teeth and luckily they were still there, but when I pulled my hand back it was covered in blood and I could tell that my lip was slashed open.

Our team had so many people hurt I knew I needed to stay on the floor, but the medical staff forced me to come off. I was furious. When we got to the locker room I looked in the mirror and saw there was a hole clear through my mouth. I could literally put my finger through my lip. I was looking at myself and I was mad because I knew this was my time. I had worked so hard to get to this moment, to be in a playoff game against the defending champions and I thought, *C'mon Nate, don't let this moment get taken away from you.*

I wanted to punch the mirror but I couldn't afford to also hurt my hands, so I threw some towels around to release some of that emotion. I could hear the crowd in the arena and I knew my teammates were out there, battling without me, and I was going to do whatever I could to get back into the trenches with them. That's the only thing I thought about. I know I bounced around in my career and come off the bench for most of it, but I always told myself that if I ever got 'starter minutes' I'd perform at a high level. And here I was, starting for the Chicago Bulls, on the biggest stage, getting starter minutes. I was talking to myself in my head, challenging myself.

I said, *Nate, here it is. The moment you've been waiting for. You've had to prove yourself your whole career and you know how good you can be. This is the biggest platform you could ask for. This is the playoffs— against the best player in the NBA and the best team in the NBA. God is putting this right in front of your face and it's time you show the world what you can do.*

This conversation ran through my head as the pain shot through my mouth. After a little while, I talked myself out of feeling the injury. I really did. I've always believed in talking to yourself to get through things. If you tell yourself enough times that you can do something, you do it. This time, I talked myself out of caring about the gash in my lip and I told the medical team, "Hurry up. Let's get stitched up and continue to battle."

I got five stiches on top and five on bottom, but my mouth wouldn't stop bleeding. When halftime ended I was still leaking blood and my face was still swelling, but they gave me some stuff—which really burned—to keep the blood from pouring out of my mouth and I was able to go back out on the court.

When I stepped on the floor of American Airlines Arena in Miami after halftime, the game was tied. Before the game, LeBron James was given the league MVP award and I remember thinking, *This is the perfect night for us to win. He might be the MVP, but we're going to play harder and tougher and win this game in his house.*

Once play started in the third quarter, I forgot about my banged-up face and the rip in my lip and I put everything I had into getting my teammates involved, keeping our energy up and getting buckets. I didn't care if I got hit again.

We were down four points late in the third quarter after a few great plays by LeBron and Dwyane Wade, and I knew we had to get some points to keep them from getting momentum. With about thirty seconds left in the third, I took a quick handoff from Joakim Noah and knocked down a deep three to make it a one-point game. When the ball went through the net, I started nodding my head, feeling it. I was telling Miami that we were still here—and we weren't going anywhere.

LeBron crushed a dunk about halfway through the fourth quarter and the Heat were still ahead. We had a lot of our best players on the sideline with injuries—Derrick Rose, Luol Deng, Kirk Hinrich—but me and Joakim Noah and Carlos Boozer and the younger guys, we wouldn't let up.

We traded buckets for a little while until it was all tied up at 86 with a minute and a half left in the game.

I knew this was our moment. We either seize the game and get the win or they take it from us. The next time we got the ball I hit a step-back jumper at the top of the key to put us up two. I remember our bench was going off and I just walked back nice and calm and smiling, like I knew what was about to happen.

Miami missed their next shot, and when we crossed half-court I saw that I had Ray Allen on me. Ray and I go way back, which I'll get to later, but at that moment, he was just a guy who wasn't fast enough to guard me. I kept up my speed and took him with one dribble, going right by him to the hoop for a floater to put us up two baskets.

Now we're up four with under a minute to play on the road, and when I look across the court I can tell that LeBron and Wade and Chris Bosh are trying to gather themselves. On the next possession, LeBron shot an air ball. We took possession and once we got the ball past half-court, I felt like one shot would put it away—and I was feeling it. I knocked down another three and the game was over. They were stunned. The arena was silent. We just did the impossible.

We beat the Miami Heat on their home court in the playoffs.

After we celebrated for a bit and things were winding down with my teammates, I had time to relax. I was lounging, watching SportsCenter with an icepack on my face, when I finally turned on my phone, which I shut off earlier in the day to avoid distractions. I had fifty missed calls and a couple hundred texts waiting for me. My phone was blowing up trying to load everything and I was getting notifications that I was a trending topic on Twitter. I kept thinking, *Wow.*

We ended up losing that series, but that night and the next day—and really ever since—I've gotten so many tweets and letters from kids who were told they were too short or too small to do stuff, and telling me how I inspired them. I even get letters from parents telling me how much their kids look up to me. I remember one letter said, "Thank you so much, Nate. You make my son a believer that he can do anything in this world if he convinces himself that he can do it and if he works as hard as Nate Robinson."

That's the beauty of this game for me. I can reach people and inspire people by how I play. And that was the beauty of that Bulls team. We had most of our starters hurt and we kept on playing with everything we had. We risked it all. That's what I kept telling my teammates in the huddle of our games during the first-round series against Brooklyn and then against the Heat.

I'd say, "We're going to do whatever it takes. I know we're shorthanded but who cares? We're going to put it all on the line. We're going to risk it to get the biscuit."

That line, "Risk it to get the biscuit," kind of became our motto during that little playoff run. I'd get down in the huddle after a little talk and I'd yell, "You gotta risk it!" and then the rest of the guys would scream, "To get the biscuit!"

It was awesome, but that was what we had to do. We had to risk it all to win. For me, that's how I've always played; I feel like I risk everything in every game. That's why when the media interviewed me after some of my big games about my style of play and why I play so hard, I knew exactly what to say:

"God blessed me with a lot of heart and no height, and I'll take that any day."

I said it and I meant it.

But my story isn't about one game or one series. My story is about a lifetime of proving myself. It's about ignoring obstacles and using sheer will and unstoppable determination to achieve goals in sports and in life. My story is the story of overcoming physical and mental adversity to live your dream. My story begins in Seattle, where, you guessed it: I was the smallest kid on the block.

CONTENTS

PART I
STATE OF NATE

PART II
ON DUNKING

PART I

STATE OF NATE

CHAPTER ONE

BORN SHORT, RAISED TALL

I started loving basketball when I was five or six years old. My dad had a collection of VHS tapes of his favorite NBA games and his favorite players, and we'd hang out and watch tape after tape. He made me pay special attention to the little guys like Muggsy Bogues, Nate Archibald, Vinnie Johnson and Spud Webb.

My dad would say, "Look at these men. These are the guys you need to watch carefully."

I guess he knew I wasn't going to be very tall because we watched more tape on Muggsy Bogues than anyone else. Muggsy was 5'3" and I studied everything he did. I was just a little kid, but when I'd watch the tapes I swear I thought he was a little kid out there too. I had no frame of reference for all these guys being grown men. I just thought there were a few kids who were so good at basketball that the league allowed them to play in the NBA. I know that sounds strange, but I was six years old and that's what I thought.

As I got a little older and realized that guys like Muggsy and Spud Webb were grown men, I couldn't get my mind around how they could be that good against guys so much bigger. I thought, *I'm not going to be super tall, so I should model my game after these guys.*

It all changed for me when Allen Iverson came into the league in 1996. I was twelve years old. I had only been playing organized basketball for two years, but Iverson showed me what was possible. He was barely six feet tall and he could single-handedly lift teams with the way he played—his energy level and the way he carried himself. I fell in love with how he played the game of basketball.

★★★

I don't think anyone knows this, but a girl taught me how to play basketball.

My cousin Passion taught me everything I knew before I ever played organized ball or five-on-five ball or anything. She taught me how to dribble, how to shoot and how to work hard. She would wake up at six in the morning and wake me up and make me do drills with her. It was funny because she never let me shoot while she worked out. I would just rebound and pass, rebound and pass. She was showing me patience; she said if I rebounded and passed well she'd let me shoot when she was done. She's the reason I do the behind-the-back thing when I shoot my free throws. Since she used to do it, I learned it. She taught me about dedication at a very young age. It also helped that when it came to basketball, and sports in general, things just came naturally to me, like jumping. I could touch a regulation NBA backboard when I was ten years old—and I wasn't even five feet tall.

Another thing that helped me was that I was faster than all the other kids and I learned things quicker. My mom says that I was walking before I was seven months old and that I was riding a bike around age two. I have three kids of my own and I know that I did those things way earlier than they did. Since I was hitting those milestones so soon, I guess it shouldn't have been that much of a surprise that when the time came, I picked up the finer points of basketball fast as well.

Still, I can't really explain my early development, other than to say it always felt like my body was built to run and jump. I was also blessed with a strong work ethic for things I liked, which allowed me to spend hours practicing sports without a break when other kids would get bored. When you combine those things, it gave me an edge over kids my age, even though I was usually smaller.

The one thing I do know is that I got my athleticism from my dad. He was a star running back at the University of Washington and was the MVP of two Rose Bowls. He was drafted by the Buffalo Bills but didn't really play much in the NFL.

★★★

Even though I was a gifted athlete for a little kid, I spent the early part of my childhood messing around on driveways and playgrounds. It wasn't until I got to fifth grade that I joined my first basketball team, when my friend's dad, Joe Perry, or Uncle Joe as we all called him, asked me to join the team he was coaching called the Mean Machine.

Uncle Joe wasn't just some neighborhood guy who decided to coach. He was about 6'9" and played in the NBA for a little bit. He really opened my eyes as to how much you could love a game because I watched him dedicate his life to hoops day-in and day-out. He was special.

I can close my eyes right now and picture what he looked like back then. The best way to describe him is to say that he looked like Bill Russell without the beard—and he preached the fundamentals like Russell too. He taught us everything about passing, sharing the ball, about keeping your head up when you dribble so you can watch what's in front of you as it develops. He also taught us how to play for each other and how to make sure everyone had fun. His goal was to win and make sure every kid was happy.

The guys on that team were my first real teammates and I learned so much from them. One kid, Andy, had great handles and was so quick. I had to play against him every day, and even at that young age I learned how to use practice to get better. I also learned what it was like to have a dominant big man on your team. We had a big kid we called Akeem the Dream. We'd just throw the ball into the post and let him work. After all my time on the playground, where I shot as much as I wanted, playing with Akeem showed me that when you have an advantage somewhere on the floor, you have to use it. It was a valuable lesson I'd carry with me all the way to the NBA.

While we didn't have too many problems on the court, there were some real-world issues off the court that made things difficult for us. For one thing, some of the kids on the team were poor and didn't have bus money to get to games or practices. Uncle Joe solved that problem by driving around and picking up every kid on the team himself.

Looking back on that now, I realize he made so much about the Mean Machines possible. We were all young kids, but when we saw what he was doing for us, and the way he committed himself to making sure we could play and practice, it was impossible for that attitude not to rub off on us. Plus, he was always talking about teamwork and sticking together. He'd even put us in games that he knew we'd lose just to build our sense of camaraderie.

He'd set up scrimmages for us against these older kids and say, "These young men are older than you, they're bigger than you and they're faster than you. They might be better than you in every way, but you guys can beat them if you learn how to do it together and to count on each other."

But Uncle Joe wasn't the only one who was teaching me about life. After every game, each kid would get a snack pack with oranges and Capri Suns and snacks. I was young, but even at that age I recognized what was going on because my mom made those snack packs a lot of the time and I remember being in the kitchen helping her make them. It was extraordinary.

There were nights when kids from my Mean Machines team and kids from my brother's team and girls from my sister's cheerleading squad were all at our house for snacks because my mom wanted to make sure all the kids could eat something after they played. I'd look around and see my mom working to get everyone food and making sure kids were okay and I couldn't believe all that she did. I mean, I lived in a one-bedroom apartment with my mom and my brother and sister, and here she is hosting fifty kids without asking for help or anything.

I was getting a real-world education, learning about teamwork on the court from Uncle Joe and learning about sacrifice and selflessness from my mom at home. It was a great environment for me and it allowed me to focus on basketball.

★★★

Once I started practicing on Mean Machine and listening to Uncle Joe, the game truly opened up for me. It was like all of the tapes I watched with my dad and all of the games I watched with my brother and all of the NBA video games I played with my friends finally came together. I wasn't just a kid on the driveway shooting and doing moves around imaginary defenders or my little brother and sister. I was out there, playing, putting points on a real scoreboard and showing people what I could do. And I'll be honest—and I'm not afraid to say this because it's the truth, even though I might sound cocky—I was good. I could dribble and shoot with my right hand and left hand. I could sky through the air and grab rebounds over kids much taller than me. The whole game just clicked for me, especially on offense.

When it came to defense, I remember the first game I was asked to play lock-down D like one of my Seattle favorites, Gary Payton.

We were playing a team with a star on it and Uncle Joe told me to try to shut him down with good defense. At the time, I was really focused on offense and scoring, but my team needed me to play defense and I made it my mission that night to stop their best player.

As soon as the ball was tipped, I was on the guy, who was probably four inches taller than me. I figured out that if I read his eyes I could see where he was going to pass the ball before he passed it, and the next thing I knew I was getting steals left and right. I learned that if I watched his hips I could see which way he was going before he actually went there and I was able to knock away his dribble. Once I just took the ball away when he went to put it on the floor. Nobody my age was doing this stuff, but like I said, it just came to me. I felt like there was nothing I couldn't do out there. I averaged over 25 points a game as the smallest guy on the floor. And I was a showman too, just like some of my favorite athletes.

I loved Michael Jordan like most kids, but my two favorite players in any sport at that time were Deion Sanders and Barry Sanders. When I stayed with my dad it was mandatory that we watched football on Sundays, and he'd always get extra excited when Deion and Barry were playing.

Once I watched Deion, I couldn't get enough of him. I had my dad tape specials on him and his time at Florida State. I started wearing number two because Deion wore that at Florida State.

Prime Time. Neon Deion. I ate it all up. When I started playing football the next year I copied everything he did, but on Mean Machine I just wanted to get the crowd going like he did.

We went undefeated that season and never even gave up a lead until we got to the city championship game, where, out of nowhere, we found ourselves getting beat badly at halftime. We were all little kids and we'd never even been behind before—let alone in a title game—and my teammates weren't handling it well. Guys were crying and pouting and I just felt something inside me turn. I wasn't going to let us have this negative attitude, and I had no doubt we would win that game.

I realize it sounds like a mature thing for a ten-year-old to do, but I just started firing guys up.

"We are not giving up, guys!" I shouted. "You want to cry, then cry, but I want to win a championship! I know we can win it. I know it! I'm not giving up! Are you guys? You guys want to give up? I didn't think so! Now let's get out there and get it done! Let's go out there right now and play for each other and win the championship!"

The guys all started shouting and we went out there and we took it to them in the second half and we won. I've done that a thousand times in my career since, even when I was in the playoffs with Chicago, which I'll get to later. I don't know where it came from. I just felt responsible for those guys.

I don't remember if at the time any of my teammates had younger brothers and sisters to look out for, but I did. I was in charge of my little brother and sister. Every day I had to make sure my brother and sister got home from school, and every day I'd walk them all the way to their practices and I'd have to take my sister to a program upstairs at the facility so she could do her homework while we practiced. Then I'd have to stay and do my homework while my brother practiced and then I'd walk us all home.

Some kids would try to bully us on the way home and I'd have to fight occasionally to stick up for us. I did what I could to show them how to take care of themselves. We didn't have an older brother and my mom worked a lot, and we didn't see my dad all the time so that kind of protective stuff was up to me. I did what I could as a ten-year-old and I think that's what made me feel so responsible for my basketball team. I really felt like it was my job to show us we could do it.

After the win Uncle Joe took us out for pizza and soda and we had a great time. I still see some of the guys from that team today. Our kids play together. It's a bond we'll share forever.

★★★

One of the earliest lessons I learned in life was that the only problem with loving something as much as I loved basketball is that it can be taken away from you. In my case, after we won the championship with Uncle Joe, I wasn't allowed to play on the team the next year because of poor behavior. I don't know if I had ADHD or I was just a hyper kid, but I was always getting in trouble trying to be the class clown. I never understood why there was a problem because my grades were good; I just liked to have fun while I was in school.

I was the kind of kid who would ask to go to the bathroom, and then on the way, if there was a classroom door open or something, I would start dancing or goofing off or I'd throw a piece of paper at a friend and run away. My dad would yell at me and say stuff like, "There's a time to play and there's a time where you have to get serious and do work."

I understand that now, especially as a father, but back then it didn't register with me at all. I wanted to have fun. Always. Eventually, that mindset got me into detention once, then twice, then pretty much every day to the point of me practically living there.

We had an honor system in school for behavior and I had to stay above a certain level to be able to play basketball, and it seemed like I could never do it. I'd play one game, get in trouble, miss a bunch of games, then play one more. I think I maybe got to play in five games. And it hurt so much to miss the games because we were good, but my head wasn't into the idea that it was a privilege to play hoops for the school. I thought it was my right because I loved it. This led me to the first time I had to sacrifice something to play.

The team made the championship game that year against a much better school and I wasn't supposed to be allowed to play.

The whole week leading up to the game I just kept thinking to myself, *This is the championship game. I'm playing. There's no way I'm not playing.*

I finally talked my coach into letting me play, but I knew if I played I'd have to eventually face the principal and deal with the consequences. At that point, I didn't care. I felt like my teammates needed me and I had to do what was necessary to get on the court.

We played our hearts out but we ended up losing by three or four points. And I ended up losing pretty much every Saturday for the rest of the school year.

After the game I met with the principal, who was really mad that I played since I wasn't eligible according to the honor system. He told me that he understood how much I loved basketball, but that there had to be a price to pay for not following the rules and for acting out. He told me that since I played when I shouldn't have, I would have to attend Saturday detentions for the rest of the school year. He also made me clean the gym, walk all over school and pick up garbage and do all kinds of other community service-type stuff.

When he told me what I had to do for playing in the game, I just said, "Yup, I'll do it."

It was worth it to me to have been there for my teammates. I keep that mentality to this day.

CHAPTER TWO

THE FRESHMAN PHENOM OF RAINIER BEACH

When it came to practicing basketball, I was like the Post Office: I would practice in the rain or sleet or snow. It didn't matter. All I needed was a ball and a hoop and I'd be working on my game somehow. One day when I was in the eighth grade, I was practicing against the corner of my house, just doing all these moves I saw NBA guys do. I used to imagine the toughest defenders and I would slice them up, working on my crossover, my step-back jumper, my behind-the-back dribble drive—everything.

On this particular day, it was pouring rain and I was still out there killing it, when a car pulled up across the street to drop off a kid at his house. The man at the wheel stopped and watched me play for a few minutes. Then he rolled down his window.

"What's your name?" he asked me.

"I'm Nate," I said.

"What high school do you go to?" he asked.

"I'm in eighth grade," I said.

"What!?" he shouted. "For real?"

"Seriously," I said. "I'm only thirteen."

"You should come play for me next year in high school at Rainier Beach," he said.

"Who are you?" I asked.

"I'm the head basketball coach, Mike Bethea," he said. "You should come down and watch us play."

Growing up where I grew up, I had heard of Coach Bethea. He was a high school hoops legend. And here he was, after watching me mess around on the side of my house for five minutes, asking me to come play for him. I told my mom about the conversation, she talked to him a little later, then took me to one of their games a few weeks later.

When I walked into the gym, the game had already started and the place was packed. It took about two seconds to figure out who the best player was. This guy was doing moves behind his back, dunking, draining threes, throwing alley-oop passes and lobs and just dominating the other team. My first thought was, *Who is this guy?!*

It turns out that guy was Jamal Crawford. Jamal has been in the NBA for about twelve years and is one of the best scorers I have ever seen. The amazing thing is that when I saw him that first game, he was only a junior in high school.

I talked to my friends in class the next day and told them all about him. Then I said, "I know where I'm going to high school: Rainier Beach."

I was so fired up at the thought of joining Jamal the next year, but there was one problem: I was scheduled to go to Garfield High School like the rest of my family.

When I told my mom what I wanted to do, she resisted the idea of me going anywhere but Garfield. At first. Like I said, she went there and practically everyone in my family went there. I remember telling my mom, "I don't want to go to Garfield. I want to go to Rainier Beach and start my own legacy."

The other thing was that we actually lived right down the street from Rainier. I could pretty much walk there. My mom finally agreed and when I called Coach Mike to tell him, he said, "Get ready to play on the varsity team as a freshman."

★★★

High school was really the first time that I started to get made fun of for being short. I guess up until then I was short, but since most of the other kids were still only in middle school, nobody was really that much taller than me. When I stepped on the basketball court for the first time as a freshman, I was only about 5'4". The second shortest guy on the team was about 5'8" and everyone else was way over six feet.

Guys would mock me and call me every name in the book for being short, but I really didn't let it bother me. I think what allowed me to get through it was how I carried myself. I knew I was better than every single guy on the freshman team and I knew that my real competition was with the older guys. I even felt that way in eighth grade when we'd play in summer leagues. I just knew how good I could be and I carried myself like I belonged with the best. But even though I felt that way, I wasn't just handed a spot on the team. Coach Mike wanted to see how I would do against everybody, so at first he put me with the freshmen. This didn't last long because I was too good to play with them.

Then he tried me with the junior varsity team, and even though most of those guys played varsity too I was still dominating, so he put me on both the JV and varsity.

When the season started, I would play two quarters of JV and then I'd play varsity either later that night or the next day. JV was fun, but it was just a way to get in a warm-up. Most of the times in the two quarters I played to stay eligible for varsity I would have 25-30 points.

I definitely had to pay my dues on varsity as a freshman, but very early on Coach Mike told me he saw something special in me. He'd say, "Nate, you can be anything you want to be. You have something that nobody else has. It's a gift. I see it in your eyes. I've never seen anyone with the eye of the tiger that you have."

I'll never forget that. But if I'm totally honest, at the time I thought basketball was my second best sport. I even told Coach Mike. I used to say, "I play basketball for fun, but I'm a football player."

The freshman football coach also said I could play varsity, but there were some huge guys playing varsity ball and I was just too small.

Meanwhile, I learned a lot about high school basketball and how to play on a real team that year from Coach Mike and from Jamal. Jamal was getting recruited and scouted by almost every major college program and I watched how he handled it all, which I'll get to later.

We had some games where coaches from Duke, North Carolina, Michigan and Ohio State would be sitting in the stands watching us play. I was only fourteen years old and I had seen most of those coaches on TV during the NCAA tournament. It was crazy.

Jamal had an incredible year and we went to the playoffs, but ended up getting only seventh in the state. When the season was over, I told Coach Mike that I was going to work on my game and that next year, as a sophomore, I didn't want to play JV and varsity. No more bouncing around. I wanted to play just varsity. He told me he had no problem with that if I was good enough.

After basketball I ran track, and that summer my dad worked with me on finding my true jump shot.

"You need to learn how to shoot," he said. "You have all the speed and quickness a basketball player could ask for. You just need to be able to knock down your shot all the time."

He signed me up for some shooting camps and we worked all June and July on my form and on my rotation. After a few months of shooting what felt like a million balls with perfect form, one day I was out there stroking it and I knew I had it. I could just feel that everything was in tune and I didn't have to think about it anymore. All the hard work paid off. My dad saw me shooting and he was so proud.

"You're going to be unstoppable," he said. "Now you can add a complete offensive game to your driving and dunking. With everything you can do, you just need to go out there and do it. Be the best you can be. You just need to believe in yourself. You're Nate the Great."

My dad helped me get that mentality to always believe in myself.

★★★

When school came back around in the fall, I went in for my physical and saw that I had grown about five inches! I remember talking to the nurse after she measured my height, which was 5'9" going into my sophomore year, and I said to her, "I have one more growth spurt in me. My dad is 6'1" and I'm going to shoot up another three or four inches by the time I'm a senior."

The nurse just looked at me and said, "Nate, you're done growing. I'm sorry."

"No way," I said. "I'm only fifteen."

"I'm telling you," she said. "You come back to me your senior year and I promise, you'll be 5'9"."

I still don't know how she knew this, but she was right. I'm the same height right now that I was my sophomore year in high school. Every summer I would go for my physical and watch them

measure my height and it was always the same: 5'9", 5'9", 5'9"...
Even in college I kept hoping for a few more inches. I knew plenty
of guys who grew three or four inches at nineteen or twenty years
old. But not me. My mom is short so I guess I got the short gene.
I was 5'9" then and I'm 5'9" now.

Thanks to all of my hard work that summer, I met my goal of
playing only varsity as a sophomore. Our team was awesome. Me
and the twins, Lodrick and Rodrick Stewart, who were already
6'4" as sophomores, came off the bench and lit it up. I could already
dunk easily in practice, but that year I got my first dunk in a game,
which is something people ask me about all the time because I'm
known for my three NBA dunk contest wins.

For the record, I dunked a volleyball for the first time when
I was in eighth grade and I dunked a basketball for the first time
in a game my sophomore year. The dunk happened on an out-of-
bounds alley-oop play and the gym exploded. Nobody expected
it. Even the other team's fans went crazy. It was just awesome.

I probably could have dunked earlier but I have small hands,
so at the time I needed to either cuff the ball or dunk it off a pass.
That first dunk put me on the map as a basketball player in Seattle.
At the time I was best known for football, but once people heard I
could dunk and started hearing about all the other things I could
do on the court, the basketball talk really picked up.

We finished third in the state that year and almost the entire
team played on the Gary Payton All-Stars AAU team that
summer. I'll never forget it because we won every tournament
we were in and I was just coming into my own as a legitimate
basketball player. To that point, I had always thought about playing
football in college because I was really making a name for myself
as a cornerback and multi-position guy on offense, but I couldn't
ignore the fact that I was scoring almost forty points a night in

these AAU games against the best players in the state. After that summer, I realized I wanted to play college basketball too.

Then the bottom dropped out and I pretty much didn't play sports for year.

CHAPTER THREE

NO HOOPS, NO JOY IN OAKLAND

Toward the end of my sophomore year in high school I could feel that I was going to have a monster junior year. I was putting on muscle, and all of the sports I loved were getting easier and easier for me with all the work I was putting in. The teams I was on were good and I knew we'd be playing for state titles. Also, my younger brother was going to be a freshman and we were going to get to live our dream of playing on the same high school team. Things could not have looked better. Then I got a phone call, and the worst year of my life began.

The call was from my dad, who told me that I had to move to Oakland to live with him and help out with my family. My Uncle Lights had diabetes and my dad, who had other little kids in Oakland, needed help taking care of him. He told me that my family needed me and there was nothing I could do about it.

I loved my Uncle Lights, but I was a junior in high school and all of my family and all of my friends and everything I knew was back in Seattle and I didn't want to go. I cried and cried and was so mad my dad was robbing me of being in high school with my brother.

My dad enrolled me in James Logan High School in Oakland and that was it. Done deal.

If there was any silver lining to being there it was that I got to spend lots of time with my Uncle Lights when he really needed me. He was a pastor, so every Sunday I would drive him all the way to San Francisco in his van to help set up his church. There would be days when it was just the two of us, talking about life the whole way there and then, if nobody showed up, which happened a lot, doing the whole service together.

We'd even have communion with just the two of us.

"When you're praying to the Lord, all you need is two or more people and he's in your presence," he'd tell me.

I'll never forget that. There were plenty of days when we'd have thirty or forty people there, but sometimes we'd have just six or seven. Every Sunday I'd listen to him talk and no matter how many people were there, he'd say to me just beforehand, "Let's pray, get scripture, and go eat some breakfast."

He was the kind of guy who would give this really serious, purposeful sermon in one minute and then be cussing like a sailor and telling you a dirty joke the next. He knew he wasn't perfect but he lived his life by doing everything the right way by God, and he didn't think swearing was something that mattered. He was just so comfortable in his own skin, which is why he was one of the first people to really preach to me how important it was for me to be comfortable in *my own* skin. In addition to having long talks with me, the other thing Uncle Lights enjoyed doing was watching me play basketball.

"Never let anyone tell you how good you can be," he'd say. "You gotta always swing for the fences and show people how good you are. When you get a chance, go to the lane, dunk on people, show no mercy. When you're hot, shoot and keep shooting and show the world what you can do. Show them your energy and passion. The world needs energy and passion. Don't hold anything back."

When I think about my uncle now, I realize that he was the first one to really give a voice to how I felt about myself. So many things he told me stay with me to this day.

"Don't be afraid to be who you are, even if people don't like you," he'd tell me. "In this world, there are going to be people who hate you. There are going to be people will try to bring you down. There are even going to be people who pretend to like you, but they really don't. All you have to be is you, and you'll know who the people who really care about you are. Those are the only people whose opinions matter."

Even after I moved away from Oakland, we stayed close and I'd go down to visit him in the hospital all the time. It was so hard to watch him go through the stages of diabetes. Once he got really sick they had to amputate his legs, then his hands. It was like they were slowly taking little bits and pieces of him.

In between his hospital visits, when I was a little older and in the NBA, he'd come to my games in Oakland in a wheelchair and he'd say all kinds of goofy things. He just wanted to make me laugh.

One time I was talking to him before a game and he was busting on me, saying, "Nate the Great, Your Booty Stank."

He used to say that when I was a little kid, but he kept saying it at the arena, making me laugh.

"I'm a grown man now," I told him. "You're still saying the same thing."

"Well, your booty still stank!" he said, laughing. Then he pulled me close and said, "I love you. I see you as my little 'Nate the Great Your Booty Stank' forever."

We had a very emotional bond, because during the time I was in Oakland I had to do everything for him. I had to help him in and out of his wheelchair, I had to give him baths and change his clothes and wipe his nose. There were times when he couldn't control anything, but I was there for him.

Once he got his first fake leg, he was always trying to surprise me and hit me with it. Even going through all of the hardship he was going through, he still tried to keep a smile on his face and put one on mine. I think of him whenever I'm going through tough times.

★★★

Unfortunately, when I wasn't taking care of my uncle on weekends and at night, I still had to go to a new high school where I didn't know anybody. I also couldn't stop thinking about all of my friends at Rainier Beach, and my mom and my brother and my sister and my teammates. This was supposed to be the best year of my life, and other than my time with my uncle, it was the worst.

I hated my new high school and I just didn't care. I played only the first half of the football season because I let my negative attitude affect me so much that I started to get Ds and Fs. I think I was subconsciously hoping to get kicked out so I could go home. But my dad was having none of it.

He'd give me a whooping for my bad grades and I'd just take it. It's hard to talk about how much of a depressed mindset I had, but I wasn't playing football anymore and that hurt. Plus, if I was in Seattle, I would have been a superstar on the Rainier Beach basketball team, and here in Oakland I wasn't even on my new high school's team because of my grades. The thing was, I knew that if I played at James Logan, I would have been the best player in both football and basketball, but I just didn't want it. I was so negative and in a stalemate with my dad, where he would keep whooping me and punishing me and I'd just keep taking it without trying to get better. In my head, I thought that a butt whooping would only last so long and that he'd get tired of it.

He was thinking differently.

"Nate, one day you're going to get tired of getting punished and realize that all you have to do is work hard, get good grades and you can do what you want."

Again, I was thinking that I didn't want to work hard if it meant I still had to live in Oakland. It was a tough time. All I really did for fun was play basketball at lunchtime and in my free time by myself at parks. Not being a part of a team hurt me more than you can imagine.

Then one day I was shooting around at lunch and a few kids who were on the high school basketball team came in to play with me and I just started schooling them. Nobody there had ever seen me play and I started knocking down threes and dunking and swatting shots. It was nice to feel like that again. That night I went home and decided that I had to show these California boys what Seattle ball was all about. I made up my mind that being a depressed kid with bad grades who didn't play any sports just wasn't what I was all about. I was going to make the best of my situation and that night I started studying.

Within a few months I had fixed my grades and I was getting all As and Bs.

"I told you that you can do it," my dad said.

He was so mad at me because I had wasted the first part of my junior year by slacking off. I was also mad at myself for letting my mind get to such a dark place.

Either way, I got my grades up fast enough so that I could run track and after only a few months of training I made it all the way to the state finals. I got smoked, but it felt good to be a part of something again.

Finally, at the end of spring, my dad sat me down and said, "Son, I have some good news for you. You're going to go back to Seattle."

I was so excited I almost cried. I called my mom and all my friends and told them I was coming home in the summer. From that day on I had my bounce back. My grades were awesome and I counted down the days to go back to Rainier Beach.

CHAPTER FOUR

BACK IN SEATTLE, BACK IN THE SPOTLIGHT

The second I got back to Rainier Beach I reunited with my friends and my AAU team. I had a new lease on life. I hadn't played organized ball in so long that I played every game like it was the championship. I was just flat-out driven. Every game I played I was scoring thirty points or forty points or sometimes fifty. I was on a mission.

As the big games piled up the buzz about me started building in local papers. The writers were saying that because I was back in town Rainier Beach High School was going to be a force in both football and basketball.

Most people know me for basketball now, but back in high school my whole reputation was built on football. I was a shutdown corner and I played almost every position on offense. My senior year I scored 21 touchdowns while rushing for over 1,200 yards and receiving over 500 yards. But defense was my specialty. I loved playing corner just like my one of my favorite athletes of all time, Deion Sanders.

As basketball season approached, I really had to maintain focus on football because all my friends who played only basketball were traveling to play in tournaments and I was still on the football field. Fortunately, my focus paid off because at the end of my senior year I was named the Seattle Times Class AAA State Football Player of the Year, which put me at the top of a bunch of recruiting websites' lists for cornerbacks. I was also a SuperPrep All-American in 2001.

With that kind of attention on me throughout the year, I had to pay extra attention to my grades and work on my SAT score. I had learned my lesson about taking sports for granted, and now that I had them back I wasn't going to lose them again for not doing my class work. I also knew that if I wanted to get scholarship offers to play in college I'd have to have good test scores, so my mom saved some money and was able to enroll me in the Princeton Review. I think I was in that program for six months. I went three days a week, including Saturdays, because I didn't want my scores to be an issue for any school.

Every Monday and Wednesday I would go from school to practice to Princeton Review. I was always so tired by the time I'd get to the Review, but I kept telling myself that if I wanted to make it to the NFL or the NBA I would have to go to college, and I didn't want to go the junior college route. I wanted to go right to a major program and show people what I could do, so I did everything it took to study.

In the meantime, I was getting all the motivation I needed from my mailbox because recruiting letters were coming in for football every day. It was cool. I was getting mail from Notre Dame, Texas, Texas A&M, Tennessee, Mississippi State, everywhere. The only school I didn't get any letters from was the one place I thought I really wanted to go: Florida State. I knew it was a longshot so I sent them my highlight tape but I never heard back.

UCLA and Arizona State both offered me scholarships but they were Adidas schools and I didn't want to wear Adidas. I was a

Nike guy even back then because of Michael Jordan, and I wanted to wear Nike in college. Every time I got a letter I would look to see if Nike made that school's gear.

Eventually, it came time to visit schools and I took a bunch of trips. One of my most memorable visits was to USC, where Pete Carroll, now head coach for my hometown, Super Bowl-winning Seattle Seahawks, was the head coach. He was a great guy and he told me that he wanted me to play all over the field. He said that I could just be an athlete out there, which was fine with me – but there was one problem. He didn't want me to play basketball.

I still had a great time on my visit because future Pittsburgh Steelers legend Troy Polamalu was my host. He took me all around Los Angeles and to all these restaurants and to the best spots on campus. I had so much fun.

When it came time for the official recruiting part of the visit, they showed me highlight tapes of the team and their star running backs Reggie Bush and LenDale White. Troy told me about how many awesome guys they had coming back. I could tell that they had an amazing recruiting class and were going to be a great team, but I wanted to keep the door open to play basketball so I said no.

After visiting some other schools, including Arizona State, where I was hosted by future Pro Bowler and Super Bowl champion Terrell Suggs, I decided I was going to wait until my high school basketball season was over to make my final decision.

★★★

Our basketball team at Rainer Beach my senior year was unstoppable. We lost only one game all year and we were like a freight train. Between me and twins Lodrick and Rodrick Stewart, nobody could match up with us. I averaged about 18 points, 7 rebounds, 7 assists and 3 steals that year, and we were must-see entertainment. In addition to the crowds we were drawing, nearly every major program was sending scouts and coaches to watch the twins play.

At the time, I was really only being recruited for football by big schools, but when scouts would come to watch the twins, they'd ask, "Who's the little guy scoring thirty points and dunking on everybody?"

My coach would always answer, "That's Nate Robinson. He's a good basketball player but a phenomenal football player. He just plays basketball for fun."

What he said was true, but some of those college coaches started talking to him about my interest in playing college basketball. I had kept that option open even though I didn't know if it would be possible. Then I started getting serious letters of interest.

The first big-time letter I got for college basketball was from Michigan. One of the scouts who had been to Rainier to watch Jamal Crawford play remembered me as a freshman and decided to visit to see how I was doing as a senior. He obviously liked what he saw because I got a letter from them and I couldn't believe it.

"Mom, look at this!" I shouted when I got it out of the mailbox. "Michigan wants me to play ball for them."

"Football?" she asked.

"No, basketball!" I shouted.

I really could not believe it. Then things started to snowball. All these coaches from North Carolina and Duke and Connecticut and other schools who were coming to see the twins started noticing me. I'm not saying these schools were offering me scholarships, but they were gauging my interest and that got more schools involved.

As the recruiting letters poured in that year, our wins piled up and we blew out another high school for the Class AAA State Championship. I was MVP of the tournament, averaging over 25 points a game. Our team ended up ranked seventh nationally by

USA Today and I was named Class AAA Basketball Player of the Year, which meant I got player of the year in both football and basketball. That was crazy. I still can't wrap my head around that.

During the tournament, more schools kept coming to watch the twins. Kansas, Arizona, you name it. They were all there trying to recruit those two. After one of the games I heard two scouts talking. They were saying the same things I heard in the beginning of the season, "Hold on, we're here for the twins, but who is this little guy? He's scoring forty a game!"

It all felt so good.

A few years later I had a huge game against the University of Arizona and their legendary coach, Lute Olsen, walked up to me after the game and said, "You're an outstanding player, Nate. How come we didn't recruit you?"

"I don't know," I said. "I think because I was more of a football player and nobody thought I was serious about playing college basketball."

"I've got to talk to our scouts about that," he said. "We can't be missing guys like you."

I was stunned. Coach Olsen is one of the best of all time and he was telling me that he wished he had recruited me to play for him. When stuff like that started happening my freshman year at Washington I began to think seriously about my future in hoops.

But getting back to my senior year, when all was said and done, I had a ton of offers to play football, but only got full-ride offers for basketball from Santa Clara, the University of San Francisco and Gonzaga.

There was nothing wrong with those schools, but because I was determined to play both football and basketball, I wanted to go to a bigger program in a major conference. That's what led me back to the University of Washington.

Very few people know this, but I actually committed to Washington without even going on an official visit.

Since I was local, both the football head coach, Rick Neuheisel, and the basketball head coach, Lorenzo Romar, knew who I was, so I set up meetings with the two of them.

When I talked to Washington's assistant head football coach, Keith Gilbertson, he just asked me, "What do you want to do here at Washington, Nate?"

"I want to do three things," I said. "I want to play offense and defense in football and I want to play basketball."

"That works for me," he said.

My meeting with Coach Romar was a little different. He had obviously heard of me and knew what I could do on the court, but he wanted to meet me to see what the hype was about. He actually came to an All-Star game I played in as well as a few other games during my season at Rainier Beach. I found out later that he really hadn't pushed anything in terms of an offer or any real interest because he heard I was going to be playing football somewhere else.

After we sat down and talked for a long time about what I wanted out of my college career, he said the funniest thing.

"Nate, there's only one thing I can think of that will keep me from giving you a scholarship to the University of Washington," he said.

"What's that?" I asked.

"Your hair," he said.

"What?" I asked.

"You need to cut your hair if you want to play for me," he said.

Back then I had braids in my hair and Coach Romar wanted a more clean- cut image.

"I don't care about this hair," I said. "I care about playing for you at Washington. I'll cut it tomorrow."

"Okay then," he said. "I'd love to have you on our team. Welcome to Washington."

And that was it. I committed to Washington the next day.

CHAPTER FIVE

HUSTLING AS A HUSKY: THE UW YEARS

The best way to describe my freshman year at Washington, especially during football season, is to explain how long a typical day was for me. I woke up most days at 6 a.m. to go to mandatory study hall before class. Then we would hit the weight room, have breakfast and then I'd go to my classes all morning. When classes were over we had our football meetings, which normally would be no big deal, but I played many different positions, so I had hours of meetings. I had one meeting for defense, one meeting for punt return, one meeting for the hands team, one meeting for kick return and the kickoff team... It was just one meeting after another.

Even though the meetings were about football, each one was basically like another class: You're sitting in a room and watching a dry erase board or a monitor and you're learning new things and being quizzed on things you're already supposed to know. That meant after getting up at the crack of dawn, I'd sit in my normal three or four classes a day for school and then another three or four for football. It ended up being eight or nine hours of sitting in a chair and absorbing information, and it started to mess with my head. I remember for a little while I thought I had narcolepsy or something because I would just fall asleep. Every few meetings I would doze off and the coaches would get upset and make me run.

I never had a problem running and I always had energy for football, but I was dead tired from sitting for eight hours a day listening to teachers and then listening to coaches. It was draining me to the point that I finally had to speak up and take myself out of a few meetings.

When the meetings were over we headed out to practice for an hour or two and that was the best part. Once I stepped onto that field my energy level surged and I would bust my butt the entire session.

After practice, when most guys hit the showers and went home to relax or get to bed early, I headed for the gym in my football gear to get my basketball shots up for an hour. Every night, no matter how exhausted I was, I made myself grab a ball and work on my game because I knew the rest of the basketball team was going through full practices and I had to keep my game solid. Most nights I wouldn't get to the gym until 8 p.m. or 9 p.m. and I'd just take off my shoulder pads, put my helmet in the corner and start shooting and working on moves until ten at night.

It was a brutal schedule but it allowed me to live my dream of being a two-sport athlete. I refused to let being tired or not having enough time get in the way of that dream.

★★★

I began my freshman football season as a back-up cornerback and special teams guy. I was flying around, making tackles and making a name for myself. It felt like I was playing every position. There were games when I would return punts, return kicks and play defense. It felt amazing because my dad played for Washington and here I was, wearing the same uniform and making plays.

In 1991, when I was six years old, the Huskies shared the national championship with Miami after an undefeated season. Everyone followed the team then. They had a monster squad with Billy Joe Hobert at quarterback and the beast, Steve Emtman, on the defensive line. He won the Lombardi Award and the Outland Trophy and was the most dominating defensive player in college that year.

The Huskies blew through the Pac-10 and then crushed Michigan in the Rose Bose Bowl that year. I remember that because my first game in a Husky uniform was against Michigan in Ann Arbor. I had never seen a place like that. There were over 110,000 people in the Big House to open the season and they were fired up.

We were ranked 11th to start the season and Michigan was 13th. The game was on national television and we lost by two points. I was thrown right into the fire for that one.

We won our next three games and kept our ranking at around 13 until we lost to California by a touchdown. Then we beat Arizona to stay in the top twenty-five. We could have been 6-0, but we were 4-2 and we lost the two games by a combined nine points. Then we were blown out by twenty points by USC and any real hopes for a major bowl went away.

The silver lining to giving up over forty points to the Trojans was that I became a starting cornerback as a true freshman and would go on to start the final six games.

The undisputed highlight of my year playing college football came during the Apple Cup, the rivalry game against the Washington State Cougars that's played every year as the last game of the regular season.

When we played that game in 2002, we had already lost four or five games and were just trying to get into a mid-level bowl. Washington State was a force that year and they were ranked third in the country heading into that game, which was at their home field in Pullman, Washington. If they beat us, they went straight to the Rose Bowl with a possible shot at a National Championship.

The Cougars were up 20-10 heading into the fourth quarter, but our quarterback Cody Pickett took us right down the field at the start of the quarter and we scored a touchdown to make it a three-point game. The crowd in Pullman was going crazy when Washington State got the ball back. They were driving down the field and then—boom—I picked off their quarterback to give us the ball.

It was a huge play considering the rivalry and everything that was on the line for them. We hit a field goal to send the game in to overtime. Then we each hit field goals to take it to second and third overtimes, until we finally won the game on a kick. That was an awesome experience. We shattered their championship hopes right on their home field.

That game helped us get in to the Sun Bowl, where we got beat by Purdue. When I had my end-of-year evaluations I thought I did pretty well. I went from back-up to starter and I had a couple interceptions, a bunch of deflections and thirty-four tackles.

The crazy thing about that year was that in between the end of the football regular season and our bowl game, I started practicing for both football and basketball and I actually played in a few basketball games that are memorable for several reasons.

★★★

My first college basketball game sticks in my mind not because of how well I played, but because I fouled out. I was playing and practicing football so much that I think the aggression from the field carried over to the basketball court. When I debuted against Wyoming, I used up my fouls quickly. I had also bulked up to about 190 pounds for football and I was kind of stocky, so that slowed me down a bit and I was unfamiliar with my own speed.

My second game was on the road against Santa Clara, and I got a little of my rhythm back and had a great all-around game. I scored 19 points and had 6 assists, 4 rebounds, 2 steals and also tried to dunk on two guys.

After the game the Santa Clara coach came up to congratulate me and said that the way I played was the reason they recruited me so hard. I thanked him and I was really flattered. Coaches don't usually do that stuff, but he just loved my energy.

After that game I played in the Sun Bowl with the football team, and then my attention turned completely to basketball. Within a few weeks of playing just hoops my weight went back down to about 175, and that was where I felt most comfortable. As I lost the weight, I worked my way into the starting lineup and started the last ten games of the season.

Up until that point I had really only played basketball in AAU tournaments or high school games in Seattle. Now that I was with a major college program, we were going all over the country and people were seeing me play for the first time. That was good in one way because I could make my mark as a player, but being in front of all new crowds gave a whole new group of people a chance to mock how short I was. And here's the thing: college fans are the most ruthless fans you could ever imagine.

These college kids on other campuses would see me in the game and they would come up with the craziest chants when I was at the foul line. People would always ask if it bothered me and I can honestly say it didn't. I would just find the biggest guy on their team and dunk on him! That would usually shut the crowd up pretty quick.

I scored in double figures in most of the games I played and I ended up leading the team in scoring average with thirteen points a game. After the season I was named to the All-Pac 10 Freshman team.

When my freshman year was over I took a little time to recover physically and mentally in the spring because I thought I was going to be playing two sports again the next season. Surprisingly, that didn't happen.

★★★

I always thought that if there was one sport I would eventually drop it would be basketball. I loved both sports, but my goal was to be a professional athlete, so after my freshman year I thought a lot about what I wanted to do. I think if you asked me at that moment whether I had a better shot at the NBA or the NFL, I would have said the NFL, but something inside me was telling me to go another way.

I started talking to my dad after the season ended about playing just basketball because I was playing so well. If I was that good without really practicing and with having to play my way into shape, how good could I be if I just focused on that one sport? We also took into account the chance of injury in football and the average career length, and basketball seemed like a smarter choice.

Still, even after talking to my dad I wanted to do both. Then Washington fired our head football coach Rick Neuheisel, and that kind of gave me the perfect chance to play just basketball. I know people had their differences with him, but I got along well with him. He told me a quote that I will never forget:

"Tough times never last, tough people do."

He said that to me in one of our conversations and then added, "And Nate, you're a tough guy. Don't ever let anybody stop you from getting what you want."

I was sad when they fired him. It gave me a bad vibe about the team and I felt so positive about basketball, so I went to talk to Coach Romar about playing only basketball. It was during our end-of-the-season meetings and he was shocked.

"Coach," I said. "I want to change my scholarship. I want to play strictly basketball and see how good we can be."

"Wow! Really?" he said. "I didn't think you'd ever leave football."

"Man, something is just telling me that basketball is the way for me right now," I said.

"Alright," he said. "Let's do it."

He took me right down to the scholarship office and figured out how to do the paperwork. Once that was all done, for the first time in as long as I could remember, I was no longer a football player.

That fact didn't really hit me too hard until late summer rolled around and it was time for summer practice and triple sessions, and I wasn't playing. I lived with a bunch of football players and I had so many friends on the team, so it was weird when the time came for them to go pick up their helmets and uniforms and I wasn't going with them.

"Nate, you aren't coming with us?" the guys asked me on the first day.

I told most of the guys that I was playing only basketball at that point, but some guys still didn't know.

"I don't play football anymore," I said. "I only play basketball."

The words sounded weird coming out of my mouth. I think the best way to describe it was that I felt naked. For so long my life had a rhythm to it that started with football and ended with basketball and now that first part wasn't there anymore.

The transition also messed with my body a little bit. I was used to bulking up for football and then cutting weight for basketball, and suddenly I'm not putting on that weight over the summer like I was used to. When I thought about it, I realized that I hadn't had a year when I just stayed the same weight and let my body sit at that weight and get comfortable for a long time. It was probably in my head, but I felt lighter and my reflexes felt a little faster.

Also, and this was a huge change, I had an entire summer and preseason to just practice basketball, which is something I never had before. It felt amazing, having all this time to devote entirely to hoops. The more I practiced, the more I realized that I had never actually considered the ceiling of my basketball abilities because my focus was always on football first, mainly because it came first on the calendar.

Without a divided mindset, I began to really think about the possibilities of how good I could be as a basketball player.

★★★

My sophomore year was the first time in my life that I started to become known more for basketball than football. Even though I had a great freshman season in both football and basketball, with only five guys on the floor in basketball, more people will notice if you play well. In this case, as a full-time starter, I was shining a spotlight on myself to other basketball teams and the media.

It was around this time when stories started to appear in the paper about my play. The thing was, it felt like all the sports writers got together to make a rule that if they were going to run a story on me, the headline had to have something to do with how short I was. Believe me, I was happy to be getting recognized and I was grateful for the attention, I just had to laugh at how every story focused on my height at some point.

My mom kept as many headlines and stories as she could. Here are a few examples:

Washington's Robinson Makes a Little Magic - USA Today, Nov. 28th, 2004

Little Big Dawg - Eugene Register Guard, Jan. 11th, 2005

Washington's Little Big Man - Denver Post, Feb. 10th, 2005

'Little Kid' Is a Big Time Ballplayer - Idaho Statesman, March 17th, 2005

Little Big Man Is in Motion - Washington Post, March 17th, 2005

Small in Size, Large in Heart, Big Time in Games - USA Today, March 19th, 2005

And that's just a small sampling. Like I said, I was happy that so many people were taking notice of how well I was playing, but I was never as focused on my height as much as the media was. Of course, I understand it; basketball is a tall man's game—I just didn't have to be tall to play it.

While I think I had a strong sophomore season overall (I led the team in scoring and was a First-Team All Pac-10 selection) there were a few games that stood out as turning points in both our season and my career.

The first one took place in the middle of the season against Oregon State.

Heading in to my sophomore year, I think we all believed that we had a real chance to make the NCAA tournament and maybe even win a game or two. You never know what can happen when a team gets hot at the right time. For some reason, in the middle of that season we started slumping. First we lost one game, then two, then three... And all of a sudden we were in the middle of a five-game losing streak and it was awful.

I hate to lose and it felt like there was nothing we could do to stop the streak. The lowest point during that time was in the sixth game when we were down 16 points to Oregon State. We were playing horribly and I couldn't take it anymore. I got in all my teammates' faces and told them how much I hated losing and how the losing was going to stop now. It was like I was back in my Mean Machine days. I kept ranting and raving and told the guys that if they were cool with losing I was going to go out there and win it myself.

I had only two points at halftime and I was playing like garbage, so it wasn't like I was killing it and nobody else was doing well. I stunk just as bad as the rest of the squad. I just felt like I had to be the one to ignite us.

I yelled and screamed and when we took the floor in the second half, I got hot quick. We battled back that entire half and I finished with 23 points, including a three at the buzzer to put us in overtime. Then we won in overtime and the season opened up for us.

The next week we swept Arizona and Arizona State at home. Arizona was ranked ninth at the time and I was amped for that game. I had 31 points and we started rolling, winning fourteen of our next sixteen games.

We finished the season at 19-14 and made it to the NCAA tournament for the first time in five years.

Unfortunately, we lost to the University of Alabama at Birmingham in the first round. It was this crazy high-scoring game where both teams scored in triple digits. We lost 102-100. I had almost thirty points. Getting in to the tournament was a great experience. You feel like if you can win one game you can win the next game and get to the Sweet Sixteen. It didn't happen for us that year, but I knew the next year was going to be big.

★★★

We had some serious talent returning for my junior year. Brandon Roy was a junior on that team and we also had Will Conroy and Tre Simmons. There was a feeling around the team that we could win the Pac-10 and maybe even a National Championship.

We started the season at the Great Alaska Shootout and beat some good teams like Utah and Oklahoma. Then we beat 19th-ranked Alabama in the championship game. I was feeling so good about my game and I was named the Most Outstanding Player of the tournament.

Around this time is when the serious talk began about me having an NBA career. The Shootout was televised and I heard from Jamal Crawford that scouts were talking about how me and Will Bynum, a short guard from Georgia Tech, were both looking like we could play in the NBA. I guess he was lighting up the East Coast and I was lighting up the West Coast. Either way, hearing that I was being considered for the NBA let me know that I made the right decision to focus on only basketball.

I led the team in scoring for the third straight year and we won the Pac-10 Tournament, which gave us a No. 1 seed in the NCAA tournament for the first time ever. A little-known fact I take pride in is that I led the team in rebounding five times that year. I think that's a very underrated part of my game. I'm not saying I could get double-digit rebounds every night; I'm simply saying I have a good feel for the ball and I get more boards than people think.

One of the biggest honors I got at the end of the year was becoming an Associated Press Third-Team All-American, even though I honestly thought I should have been on the second team. Still, it was a big deal. Chris Paul and J.J. Redick were the guards on the first team and Salim Stoudamire, Dee Brown and Luther Head were the guards on the second team. I was third team with Deron Williams and Raymond Felton.

When the NCAA tournament came around, we were a No. 1 seed, like I said, along with North Carolina, Duke and Illinois. We made it to the Sweet Sixteen and lost to Louisville. We all had foul trouble that game. We had to sit a bunch in the first half, but when I finally was able to come back in I gave it everything I had and dialed up the energy. We got a few steals, had some nice fast breaks, got a few dunks—it felt like it was all coming together. I had two dunks almost back-to-back to cut it to three and then it got away from us. Once they pulled ahead I kept thinking to myself, *It was right there, man!*

In the locker room we all figured that Louisville was going to win the whole thing since they beat us. They went to the Final Four but got rolled by Illinois. Then Illinois lost to UNC. I played against Raymond Felton and all those guys in AAU ball and I think we could have beaten them.

But none of that mattered when the Louisville game ended, as we were all crying in the locker room and icing our legs and getting dressed. We got a lot of bad calls against us in that game and I was blaming myself for not putting it aside and getting it done earlier. The NCAA tournament is funny because you get so wrapped up in the atmosphere and the pressure and the media, and then when you lose it's over so fast. Not just the tournament but the season too. For me, that was the end of my college career. It was over just like that.

★★★

When the tournament ended I went straight to my mom's house to relax. After a few days I decided that I was going to declare for the NBA Draft, so I stopped going to classes and started to get ready. When I told Coach Romar he was very supportive. He said to me, "You deserve all the success you're going to get in the NBA. Go ahead and make a name for yourself. Make us proud."

Instead of going to class that spring I got myself a trainer and began getting ready to work out for NBA teams. I worked with Washington basketball icon Steve Gordon. Gordon has worked with pretty much every Seattle-area basketball legend at one point and was on the staff of the Sonics. He knows every single thing about basketball and knows almost everyone in the game. He's also a great guy.

When I started working with him it was like going back to square one. We worked on every fundamental you can think of over and over again. We'd spend a whole day on bounce passes. Or we'd spend a day on dribbling while reading the floor. He was the perfect guy for me because even though I had success in college, I had really only been playing basketball full time for two years. I remember our first conversation.

"I just want to give you a heads-up," I told him. "I've been playing football my whole life and have only devoted the last two years to playing just basketball. I'm not your typical basketball player. I'm not totally polished."

"I got you," he said. "We'll get you ready for the league without a problem."

I can honestly say that he taught me almost everything I know about NBA basketball. By the time I made it to the league, I was a better, well-rounded player. He drilled in to me the importance of keeping my balance while forcing defenders to be off-balance. He taught me about spacing and how to think a few moves ahead to get to the spot on the floor I wanted.

He always used to joke with me about how I had to be the only guy he was training for the NBA who had barely two years of year-round basketball under his belt. When you combine that with the fact that I was only 5'9", he was so excited to work with me because that made me such a long shot for the league on paper. But here I was, killing it in workouts and killing it in practice with other prospects and with NBA guys.

All of the doubts I heard at that time from NBA circles about my ability to play were focused on my height. It didn't matter how many great games I had at Washington or how many other draft picks I outplayed in games and in camps—all that teams wanted to focus on was that I was well under six feet tall. It was nothing new for me, but at times it would get frustrating because scouts would watch a scrimmage or something where I'd be the high scorer, but I knew guys who weren't playing as well as me were going to get picked higher. I know if I was at least 6'2" or 6'3" I would have been a top-five pick easy. Scouts and GMs just don't see guys my height dominating and it makes them nervous. They don't like to draft unknowns, and I was an unknown commodity. For that reason, I was projected as maybe a late first-round or early second-round pick.

Sometimes I would ask a friend or a coach I know to share a scouting report on me and it always read something like this:

"Energy guy. Pure scorer. Can score in bunches from outside. Can drive at will. Excellent athletic ability. Above average passer. Able to create turnovers and cause problems on defense. Surprising rebounding and shot-blocking ability. 5'9". Questionable whether height will allow him to be effective in the NBA."

Now, if you take out that last part, I sound like an all-around player who could start in the NBA right out of college. But there was nothing I could do about my height. I'd get mad sometimes and think, *My height wasn't a problem in high school. It wasn't a problem in college. And since I've had tons of success against guys in AAU and in college who are now in the pros, it won't be a problem there, either.*

Still, I knew the reality of my situation so I committed to working harder than every other person who was going to be in the draft.

CHAPTER SIX

MY NEW HOME COURT: MADISON SQUARE GARDEN

Most people don't know that I went to the NBA Pre-Draft camp for the first time after my sophomore year. I was given jersey No. 16, which I thought was a sign because one of my kids was born on the 16th. My coach for that camp was Denver Nuggets icon Alex English and he was really supportive.

"Just go out there, have fun and get buckets," he told me.

He kind of turned me loose, and I averaged something like 22 points and 8 assists against the best guards in the country. The highlight of the entire experience was when Larry Bird told some people that if I went back to college, he was going to pick Washington to win the National Championship.

I could not believe he said that. That made me so excited to get back to school for my junior year. Obviously we didn't win it, but having him compliment me like that was incredible.

After I declared following my junior year, I kept in mind what he said and it gave me confidence going into my team workouts. Little did I know how many teams I'd actually work out for!

I'll save you the suspense: I worked out for 23 NBA teams. I basically took one full month and traveled around the country showing almost everyone in the league what I could do. Most of the workouts were a blur, but I'll never forget the last two.

I turned 21 on May 31st and I had completed twenty-one of the workouts. I had zig-zagged across the country and I was tired. The plan was for me to finish up in Sacramento and then fly home to Seattle. I wrapped up my workout with the Kings in the morning and I thought I did a great job. I called my agent from the airport and told him I was happy with how it went and that I couldn't wait to go home.

"Listen," he said to me. "We got you one more workout. It's with the Knicks. We'll change your flight. Just one more."

It was really inconvenient to fly from Sacramento to New York for one more workout, but I agreed. Then my flights started getting delayed. It was crazy. One hour. Two hours. Four hours. I think my original flight to New York was around two o'clock and I was still at the airport at 8 p.m. I called my agent and told him to forget the trip to the Knicks.

"I'm just going to go home," I told him. "I've played three years of college and I worked out for twenty-two teams. The draft is in two days. There is really nothing more I can do. I'm going to switch this flight to Seattle and go home."

"Trust me," he said. "Go to New York. We'll take care of it. We'll get you on the next flight out."

I finally left Sacramento at about 10:30 p.m. and I think I landed in New York at around 5:30 in the morning. I went right from the airport to my physical, team interviews and all that stuff, which took forever.

It was almost nighttime again before I actually got to play basketball for them. They knew how much I had just traveled and they offered me the chance to do the workout in the morning. I told them I was ready to go right now. I laced up my shoes for drills and one-on-one games and two-on-two games and full-court, and I absolutely torched it.

I didn't miss a shot for about the first hour. I also had the highest vertical jump of my life, at almost 48". Every single drill or test they put me through I aced. I think I broke records in their speed drills and my energy was non-stop. Even after the workout was over I stayed and shot around with both hands, talking to them. I didn't know at the time that trip would change my life.

★★★

I got home from the New York trip a day before the NBA Draft. I had plenty of conversations with my agents about where I might end up, but the truth was we really didn't know. After all of my workouts, I was still projected to go late in the first or possibly early in the second round.

The night of the draft there had to have been over 300 people at my mom's house. I think every person I ever met in Seattle was there. Family, friends, media, coaches, old teammates from high school and college—everybody.

As the first round wore on the tension kept building but I was having a good time. I had faith that I'd get taken in the first round, but my mindset was that even if I didn't, I was going to go in the second and I'd show that team what I could do and make the roster. Right before the 20th pick my agents called me.

"You are about to get drafted by the Phoenix Suns," they said. "But that's not where you're going to go. The pick is going to be traded to the Knicks. You're going to be on the Knicks."

After I got off the phone, I didn't tell anybody what I just found out. I told people it was a wrong number. I sat there and waited as the Knicks' time on the clock almost expired. With a few seconds left, David Stern walked to the podium and announced that the Knicks had taken me.

Everyone in the house went crazy! The place just erupted! I started screaming and crying, and other people were crying and I was filled with such happiness. I couldn't hear anything for a little while, and when I calmed down I looked at the TV and they were showing the best 30-second highlight tape of me ever. They showed my football plays and then some of my best basketball stuff. I could hear the announcers through the celebrating and they said the same stuff I've always heard:

"Dynamite athlete, incredible vertical, can dunk, drive, shoot and light up a scoreboard. His main weakness is his height."

I'll never forget that as long as I live. I get drafted and it's the best moment of my life, and the guys on TV are saying that they don't know how long I'll be in the league or if I'll make it at all because I'm too short. Now it's all these years later and I'm still here.

The first person I heard from on the Knicks was Isiah Thomas. He called to congratulate me.

"Nate," he told me. "I believe in you. If you were six feet tall I think you would have been the No. 1 pick in this draft. You can play like that."

That meant a lot coming from Isiah. He motivated me to come in and work as hard as I could.

I heard from Jamal Crawford, who was also on the Knicks, soon after that. Talking to him was like a dream. We were going to be the first two guys to ever play on the same high school team and the same NBA team.

The day after the draft I flew to New York City, and barely twenty-four hours after my dream of becoming an NBA player came true, I was standing next to the other guys in my draft class. Chris Paul. Deron Williams. Ray Felton. David Lee. Sean May. A lot of the guys who were just in the NCAA tournament with us were there.

The media interviews were a bit of a whirlwind and we were on a tight schedule from that point on until we finally started practicing. Even though the practices were with my new New York Knicks teammates, I didn't really feel like I had made it to the NBA until I touched the ball in my first preseason game. What I did with the ball, however, is something I'll never forget.

★★★

Sitting on the bench during my first preseason game was surreal. I couldn't believe that here I was, after all this time, playing in an NBA game in front of an NBA crowd. I could barely contain my energy while I was sitting there. I felt like I was going to explode.

When I finally got in the game I was like a jet engine out there, roaring and ready to go. About thirty seconds after I checked in I got a great steal and found myself flying down the court on a fast break. As I crossed the three-point line, I realized there was nobody in front of me, and since I was surging with adrenaline, I took off for a monster dunk...

And I missed it!

I tried to cuff the ball because Richard Jefferson was running me down. He caught me with a little foul they didn't call and I threw the ball off the rim. It hit me in the head and went all the way down to the other end of the court. I crashed to the ground and laid there like I was hurt.

I was embarrassed. I knew I should have just laid it in. All the coaches were looking at me like, "Son, what the hell were you thinking?!"

It's funny because I knew I was going to get chewed out, so I just got up and ran to the bench. My teammates were laughing at me and saying I had huge guts to go for the dunk.

I knew it was dumb, but I didn't know why it was THAT dumb.

"Do you know who your head coach is?" they asked.

"Larry Brown," I said.

"He's super tough on rookies," they said. "He's not gonna like that at all."

I didn't really know much about Coach Brown. I was twenty-one and I spent so much of my time either playing football or playing basketball I didn't get a chance to watch much NBA. I know it sounds odd to say that. All I really knew at that time was Allen Iverson. He was the guy I followed the most. I knew Coach Brown coached Iverson and that was it.

After the game, in front of the whole team, one of the coaches quieted everyone down and said, "Nate, what were you thinking on that dunk, son?"

"Do you want me to be honest with you or do you want me to lie to you?" I said.

"I want the truth, son," he said.

And then I gave the worst answer I could have possibly given.

"The first thing I thought about when I got that steal was all my friends back home," I said. "I thought all my buddies would be watching SportsCenter and they'd think it was awesome that I got a dunk in my first game. I wasn't thinking about anything else."

My teammates burst out laughing and Coach Brown gave me a few choice nicknames after that. One of them I can't repeat and the other one was The Highlight Reel.

"I'm calling you the Highlight Reel if all you're interested in is highlights," he said.

I embraced it because I knew they called Dominique Wilkins, one of the best dunkers ever, the Human Highlight Reel.

That was the first day I really felt like I was in the league—when I missed a dunk and got chewed out by Coach Brown.

That night I went home and did some research, which I probably should have done earlier, and I found out who Coach

Brown was. He won a National Championship at Kansas. He won an NBA Championship with the Detroit Pistons. It looked like he had coached half of the teams in the NBA.

I thought to myself, *What were you thinking with that dunk!?*

After that he loved to give me a hard time. Plus, I had to put up with all the usual rookie stuff. I was shagging bags, picking up the balls, getting doughnuts, dancing on the bus, singing stupid songs. I don't get embarrassed at all, so none of it bothered me. I think that's how I won over my teammates: I took all of it with a laugh and I never complained.

★★★

That first season in the NBA, my main goal was to keep my head above water. Jamal let me stay with him until I started getting paid and got myself squared away. He was like my big brother there and I've looked up to him over the years. Having a guy like that on your team who is looking out for you and who is there for you is so valuable. He really came through for me then. He was taking me around the city, showing me things to do and places to eat. He made me feel right at home, which is rare for a rookie.

On the basketball side, I honestly didn't have any specific goals other than to listen and take in as much information as I could. Whenever I got a chance to play I wanted to make my mark. I aimed for ten points and maybe two rebounds and two assists a game if I was in there long enough. But the team wasn't very good, unfortunately.

At one point Coach Brown got so fed up with the veterans that he started all the young guys and we won our first six games. There was a headline in the New York paper that said something like: Young Knicks Six and Oh.

That was awesome.

The most memorable Knicks game of that season by far was when I got to play my first game back in Seattle. That night was a dream come true. My mom raised money and bought 116 tickets for people we knew and then all of my teammates gave me their tickets, so we had hundreds of people at that game. All my friends from high school were there with my coaches and teammates. The whole Rainier Beach basketball team was there. I got to play in front of my family, my girl's family and my kids. It felt like it was my town for a night.

I also set it up so that the Rainier Beach team could come to the game early and watch our warm-ups and hang out by the court. They got to see how a real NBA team prepares.

The reason I set that up was because I remembered how much it meant to me when I was in high school and I got to be on the floor of an NBA arena.

When warm-ups were over Coach Brown went through the starting lineup in the locker room. After he named Jamal as the fourth starter, he said, "And guess what, we're going to start the Highlight Reel tonight."

I looked up and the whole team was clapping and cheering. I got so hyped up!

"Go out and have fun," he said.

That was the first time Coach Brown told me to have fun. I couldn't believe it. When they announced my name last in the arena during the introductions I felt like a boxer.

"Starting guard...Standing five feet nine inches tall...from your Washington Huskies...Seattle native...Nate...Robinson!!!!"

I got a standing ovation and the crowd blew up. It was so loud. They cheered so long I felt like I was the MVP. I really couldn't believe it. My teammates were all telling me they had never heard a crowd cheer like that before. It was one of the best experiences of my life.

We won the game and I had thirteen or fourteen points. I had a slow first half, then I hit a couple crucial threes in the second half, scoring ten in the fourth quarter. At that point I was in a groove and having a blast. I think Jamal, who was also excited to be back home, scored thirty. We took a bunch of pictures with family and friends after the game. That was the moment I first felt like a star in the league.

★★★

We lost almost sixty games that year and Larry Brown was fired. Isiah Thomas took over as head coach and for me that was a great thing. He was one of the best point guards of all time and I knew I could learn so much from him. He really showed me the way to play with my abilities and my height. Isiah is only 6'1", which made him one of the smallest players to ever dominate the NBA. We definitely had a bond there and he took a lot of time to work with me. He wouldn't just coach me; he'd play with me and actually show me moves that worked for him.

I'm not at all knocking other head coaches I've had, because I have had some great ones, but for me, the fact that Isiah would get on the floor with me and go through progressions of moves that he perfected was something special.

One of the things he worked on with me most was floaters heading to the hoop. For a guy my size, being able to drive hard but lay in a high, soft shot is important because it's easier for me to get blocked if I go straight to the basket. He spent hours talking to me about footwork, and how I could control my body by planning on which foot to jump off in certain situations. He called it controlled spontaneity.

I would drive to the hoop over and over and take off from different spots and different angles, simulating what would happen in a game, and he'd point out the most effective way to get my shot off at that spot on the floor. The stuff he knew was eye-opening. I guess that's how he averaged over 20 points and 10 assists for most of his career. He really took the time to make me a better player and I'll always be grateful to him for that.

I know some people have had issues with him over the years, but the one thing I can say is that he loved us. He loved all his guys. He got Jamal to come to New York. He drafted me. He got Wilson Chandler. He got David Lee. He got some good players. The problem was we just lost and lost and lost.

I never made it to the playoffs with the Knicks. The most games we won while I was there was 33. I was not used to losing like that. In high school we contended for state titles. At Washington we won the Pac-10, got a No. 1 seed in the tournament and went to March Madness my last two years. And now I finally get to the NBA and my team sucks. I couldn't take the losing, so I focused on improving my personal game, hoping it would help us win more.

Isiah coached us for only two years and then they brought in Mike D'Antoni. I was psyched when they brought in Coach D'Antoni because he ran a fast-paced offense with Phoenix and I thought we could take advantage of my speed. At first, things were great.

I had my best season under him in 2008-09 when I played almost thirty minutes a night. I averaged 17 points a game as well as 4 assists, 4 rebounds and over 1 steal a game. That's the kind of stat line I always envisioned I'd have if I was given those kinds of minutes. I thought for sure I'd get even more minutes the next year and really show what I could do. I felt like I had a good five years in New York and I was headed for five more.

I could not have been more wrong.

CHAPTER SEVEN

ALMOST KNOCKED DOWN BY THE KNICKS

Simply put, the 2009 and 2010 seasons with the Knicks were tough. I went from getting thirty minutes a night to not playing at all for no good reason. And when I say not playing at all, I went over a dozen games without getting on the floor. That was the hardest time in my basketball life. I wanted to quit. I wanted to go back to playing football. I wanted to do anything but be prevented from playing the game that I love.

One of the toughest things during that time was sitting on the bench game after game, knowing I could help my team but not being allowed to do it. The other thing that made it more difficult was that I was playing in the basketball mecca, Madison Square Garden. New York fans are some of the most passionate in the world and they were screaming for me all the time. I don't want to use specific names, but every game I would hear fans yelling, "This starter sucks, put Nate in!"

And when we were down in the fourth quarter, which was a lot, eventually a chant would start.

"We want Nate! We want Nate! We want Nate!"

It was so hard to hear that when I knew I was healthy and I could contribute.

If I was on a championship-caliber team and the guy ahead of me was outplaying me for a spot, I could understand if I didn't play so much. I wouldn't like it, but I'd understand it. But this was a bad team and we were stinking it up and I STILL wasn't playing? It just made no sense to me.

I know some of it was from an incident where Coach D'Antoni overheard me say something about the way we were playing on the bench to a teammate, but that didn't justify benching me for a month. I also knew I was producing from the bench and that I should have had a chance to start, but even though I never got that opportunity, I didn't complain about it.

I knew there were some political things going on, with Coach wanting to bring in his guys, or the guys he had coached in other places, but that was no reason to turn on me and vilify me. I couldn't help it if the New York fan base saw that we weren't a good team and that when I was on the floor I was making things happen.

Of course, since it was New York, the media ate it up and it became this thing between me and Coach, even though I didn't have a thing with him. All I wanted to do was play ball. My only problem was that I wasn't being allowed to play!

I called my mom a lot during that season, and in the course of our conversations I must have told her a dozen times I wanted to quit. I just couldn't understand the fact that my head coach was taking basketball away from me and making me out to be a bad guy. I've always had confidence. I've always been positive. I just couldn't shake how I was being portrayed. When I was at my lowest point, I called my mom again and she gave me the best advice ever.

"Mom, this hurts so much," I said. "I really just want to quit. You know me. You raised me. I don't feel like I'm a bad person at all but I'm being treated that way. I'm mad and angry inside all the time."

"I know, Nate," she said. "But here's what you need to do. You need to channel that energy and focus all of that frustration on being the best teammate and player you can be. You need to stop being upset and challenge yourself to kill them with kindness."

I thought for a long time about what my mom said and I knew she was right because she had been doing that her whole life. I learned from the best, and after that I reversed my whole thought process.

I made my practices my games. I showed up early. I stayed late. I played every scrimmage like it was my last game of basketball. I figured Coach D'Antoni wouldn't bench me from scrimmaging, so I had to show what I could do there.

I spent every second trying to make my teammates better and having a positive attitude with my coaches. I said "good morning" to everyone in the building with a smile on my face every day. I even made a point to say "good morning" to Coach D'Antoni, even though I knew he wanted nothing to do with me.

But even though my attitude changed, the benching continued. Five games. Ten games. It just kept going. I think it went all the way up to fourteen games. The whole time I stayed positive. I was thinking about all of the records I could set and all of the things I could do to help us win once I got back on the court.

After a while my mom called me and said she wanted to open the new year with me since I was going to be in Atlanta. We had a game against the Hawks on January 1st, so she flew out on December 31st. I remember that trip well because we ran into the Hawks' head coach at the time, Mike Woodson, at dinner and he was really cool to me.

"How's it going, Nate?" he asked. "You playing against us tomorrow?"

"Honestly, probably not," I said.

"Well, we hope you don't play because you'll probably kill us!" he said. "Good luck anyway."

I thanked him and put the thought of not playing out of my mind because I didn't want it to ruin New Year's Eve.

When the game started the next day, I was doing exactly what I'd done while I was on the bench for the past month: I was cheering on my teammates. It had been literally a month since I last played, so I wasn't expecting to get my name called. Then, all of a sudden, with a few minutes left in the first quarter, one of my teammates nudged me.

"Nate!" he shouted.

"What?" I said.

"Coach called you," he said.

"For real?" I asked.

Then I looked up and we had only four guys on the floor.

"Get out there!" he shouted.

I jumped up and tore off my warm-ups. It was strange because I was benched for so long I had not planned on playing. When I got in the game the crowd went nuts. Even on the road people knew what I was going through and wanted to see me play.

If I'm being completely honest, I have to admit that I was nervous. I had butterflies in my stomach and I felt like a rookie. I was so scared of doing something that would put me back on the bench for another month.

When play started I tried to slow everything down in my head like it was a movie.

Here it is, I said to myself. *This is the time you've been waiting for. You're going to go out and make your teammates better. Feed them the ball, but if you're open you're going to make it.*

I played hard, but nice and easy, trying to let the flow of the game come to me. I was trying to do everything right. After a little while the ball came around to me for an open shot and I knocked it down.

Okay, I thought to myself. *Now get in a rhythm.*

Next time down the court the ball came to me again and I got another bucket. My energy meter started getting higher and higher and I made a few more shots, had a few steals, made some passes, grabbed a couple of boards. I could feel that something special was happening. I had a little hesitation because I felt like the better I did the more I might show up my coach and embarrass him for benching me for that long, but I didn't let that bother me. I just stayed in my zone.

We were down 80-67 heading in to the fourth quarter and my teammates were getting hyped up. Like I said, we were losing, but they kept telling me that I should keep pushing.

Toward the end of that fourth quarter I really started lighting it up. I hit the last four shots for us, including the basket to tie it up and go to overtime.

Then, in overtime, even the Hawks' fans were cheering for me because I was torching them. I scored 11 of our 13 points in overtime and had the assist on the other basket. I was driving and hitting everything and the whole time I kept thinking, *This is perfect!*

I hit my last two shots to put us up four and that was what we won by.

When I went back to the locker room I got a standing ovation from my team. It was one of the best feelings of my life. After being benched and treated the way I was being treated, to come back like that felt incredible.

I was so emotional that I almost broke down in tears. I gave this long speech where I thanked my family and friends and teammates for sticking by me. It was like I won the Finals. I went on and on thanking people, and I even thanked Coach D'Antoni.

"Thank you for not playing me, Coach," I said. "That humbled me because you took something away from me that I love so much. I'll never let that happen again."

It was one of the best games of my life and my teammates knew what it meant to me. One of the best parts was that Jamal Crawford was on the Hawks at the time so he was there to see it.

"I guess he had 14 games built up in him," he told reporters after the game. "I've seen it since high school. When he's scoring, he's as good as the best of them."

David Lee said, "Against a great team, Nate single-handedly carried us. It was unreal to watch him play tonight."

Everyone was saying nice things about me and I was getting texts and calls from so many people who knew how hard the past month had been. They were all congratulating me for stepping up like that. It was the last great moment I had with the Knicks. Just over one month later I was traded to the Boston Celtics and began one of the most amazing experiences of my life.

CHAPTER EIGHT

PLAYING WITH LEGENDS: CELTICS MEMORIES

I found out about the trade to the Celtics when I was in the hospital with the flu. I was feeling horrible, lying in a bed with an IV in my arm, when Coach Romar from Washington gave me a call.

"Hey Nate, how you feeling?" he asked.

"I'm okay," I said.

"What do you think of Doc Rivers?" he asked.

I thought he was just calling to see how I was feeling and then he randomly asked me about Doc Rivers. I didn't know where he was going with that so I just told him I thought Doc was great.

"Doc's awesome," I said. "He's won a championship. He's coached great players. He's really good."

"Do you think you could play for him?" he asked.

"Coach, I'll play for anybody," I said. "There's only one place I won't play, and that's hell. I love hoops but I'm not going to hell to play there."

Coach Romar laughed, then he said, "You didn't hear this from me, but you're going to get a call from Doc Rivers in a minute."

"Really?" I said. "Thanks for the heads-up, Coach."

I hung up and barely a minute later I got another phone call and heard Doc's raspy voice on the other end.

"Hey Nate, it's Doc Rivers. Do you think you can play for me?" he asked.

"Definitely," I said. "Do you think I can? Do you think I'll fit in with the Celtics?"

"I know you can fit in," he said. "I just wanted to make sure you're ready."

"I'm ready, Coach," I said. "I'll do whatever you ask me to. I'll come in and do anything you need me to do."

"Okay," he said. "Then we're going to make a trade for you. Are you good with that?"

"Absolutely," I said.

"Good," he said. "The guys are ready for you. They're really excited. They think you can help this team a lot and give Rondo a breather. You might not play the minutes you're used to, but you can help us off the bench."

"Okay," I said.

After we hung up the reality hit me that I was leaving the Knicks. At first I was sad because it was the only NBA team I had ever known. I made some good friends on that team and I loved the city. Once it set in, I began to realize what an incredible opportunity this was going to be. Also, the fact that the Knicks didn't really want me and the Celtics did sealed the deal for me.

Doc didn't have to call me before the trade. The Celtics could have just traded for me and then had a meeting with me when I got there. That's when I realized Doc was a different kind of coach.

★★★

To me, the Celtics franchise was like living history. From Bill Russell to Larry Bird and Kevin McHale and Dennis Johnson to Paul Pierce and Ray Allen and Kevin Garnett, there was so much winning there you had to respect them. I had done so much losing with New York that going to a championship-level team made me giddy. All I wanted when I was with the Knicks was to be on a championship team one day, and now I had my chance.

I had played against Pierce and those guys for my entire Knicks career, but now to be sharing a locker room with them—it was like sharing a locker room with basketball gods.

They made me feel right at home from my first day on the team. It helped that I knew Ray Allen really well from when he played with the Sonics in Seattle and I was at UW.

When I first ran into him in Boston we reminisced a little bit.

"It's cool that you're here," he said. "I remember when I was with the Sonics you were all over the paper. Every day I'd read about how Nate the Great did this and Nate the Great did that. I remember all of that. Seattle really embraced you. They loved you."

It was fun to catch up with him because to all of us young kids Ray was just the smoothest guy you could meet. We used to call him the Smooth Criminal. When I was in college and we'd have open gym and run with the Sonics, he'd always ask me what my dreams were and what I was doing to reach them. He was great like that.

One time after we played them in a scrimmage he sat down with me and asked if I thought I could make it in the NBA.

"I know I can," I said. "I want to be the baddest little dude to ever play in the league. That legacy will last forever."

Those scrimmages were intense because we were a bunch of young guys trying to prove ourselves in the Pac-10 and we'd invite the whole Sonics team to come play us. Ray, Rashard Lewis, Nick

Collison, Flip Murray, Reggie Evans, Earl Watson—They'd all show up. They usually won, but we took them down a few times and the games were close most of the time.

After the games Ray would tell us stories about making "He Got Game" with Denzel Washington. He's a great storyteller. Of course, the thing we listened to him most about was shooting, because Ray Allen is probably the best pure shooter in the history of the NBA.

When I got to the Celtics, he picked up right where he left off in helping me with my shot.

"You're shooting lazy shots," he'd say to me at practice. "You need to shoot perfect, in-game shots in every shot at practice. You need to jump to the same height and release the ball at the same time in practice as you would in a game. The shot has to be exactly the same every single time."

If he saw me slack off on a shot or jump a little off the ground, he'd stop me and say, "That's not your jump shot. You don't want to shoot like that in a game, so don't shoot like it now."

Once I got into a rhythm in Boston, I followed him around and did all of the drills he did. I shot with him before games, I did his grueling treadmill workout—everything. He taught me about having a commitment to my craft. In fact, the entire Celtics organization taught me about discipline.

When I was with the Knicks, it always felt like everything was chaotic. I was having fun and doing my thing before my rough patch with Coach D'Antoni, but for the most part there was no balance or foundation or stability. I had three head coaches in barely five years, and so many players moved in and out that those of us who were there the whole time got used to things being crazy.

Once I got to Boston, I realized I was going from one of the worst-run teams to one of the best. I had to change how I did almost everything. I had to change my attitude, the way I carried myself, the way I prepared for the game—all of it. It was a total evolution for me. I went from guys hoping to win each game but not really having a season-long plan to a place that expected to win championships and took each game as one step closer to getting there. The preparation and planning was almost overwhelming. Also, the teamwork was unbelievable.

During my time with the Knicks, so many guys were involved in trade rumors and we lost so much that guys played for themselves a lot. In Boston, it was like the guys really loved each other and wanted the other guys to be awesome. I had never seen anything like it. It was refreshing. I had no idea, to that point, what it took to be a winner in the NBA.

I also had no idea how much work I would have to put in. I knew after one practice that I was going to have to hurry up and get my act together so I could contribute.

The other huge difference was having a coach like Doc. Other coaches I played for didn't command the respect from the team that Doc did. If he said something, everyone stepped in line because they knew he took them to a title before and he could do it again.

Before one of my first games I was joking with someone off to the side while Doc was talking to some players on the floor and he jumped all over me.

"Nate, we don't condone joking and laughing and giggling and not being focused on game day," he said.

"Sorry, Coach," I said.

After the game I went to him and apologized.

"Coach, you have to excuse me for that," I said. "It won't happen again. It's just that's what I've been used to my whole career in New York."

"Nate, son, we're going to have to figure out a way to channel all of that energy you have before a game to get you focused on your assignments, because I need you," he said. "I need you to be ready."

"I will be, Coach," I said.

One thing I had to get used to was how much the Celtics emphasized defense. We really didn't spend that much time on it in New York, and all of a sudden I have so many defensive assignments that Doc would stop scrimmages in the middle of a play to ask me not only where I'm supposed to be on defense but where all the other guys are supposed to be too.

It was just a whole other level than what I was used to, but I got to work quick. I started watching a ton of film and it really opened my mind as to how much I hadn't learned about the game yet.

Even on offense, Doc would stop a play in practice and ask me, "What's the name of this play? What do you do on this play if your No. 1 option isn't open? What do you do if you're double-teamed? Who gets the ball if the post is doubled?"

He would drill me until I knew every part of the playbook for every position.

In the beginning, I was behind the 8 ball the whole time. Sometimes my teammates would be helping me learn something and I'd say, "This is like going from elementary school right to college."

Since I was a point guard, I spent a lot of time with Rajon Rondo and I worked so hard to see the offense like he did, because he's brilliant. He not only knew every single play and where every guy was supposed to be on our team, he knew almost everything about every other team too. He memorized guys' tendencies and he knew their calls. He was so smart that it inspired me to try to be like that.

We started watching tape together, and I would observe how he watched games. Slowly, I started picking things up and catching on. I began to notice guys' tendencies and their moves and the percentages of times they'd go left or right or where they liked to shoot from and the angle they liked to get passes from.

The other thing I started doing, which I hadn't done before was watch film of myself to see where I could improve. That helped me so much and it allowed me to be more in tune with the game.

Then, of course, being around KG and Pierce just helped me more. Those guys were brilliant too. They knew everything they could possibly know about each other on the court and how to carry themselves off of it. With guys like that to follow, I just got in line and worked hard.

After a while, Doc pulled me aside and said, "Nate, thank you for trying so hard. I see your effort and I can see that you're getting better. I know you're taking this seriously. You're catching on."

★★★

One of the best ways to get a feel for each of the stars on that Celtics team was to study how they handled themselves in pregame.

I had heard about Kevin Garnett's intensity over the years, but you really have to see it to believe it. When it's game day he comes in, throws his stuff in his locker and gets right into his zone. I watched him over and over. When he shows up he gets dressed and then goes into the sauna and steam room. Then he lifts weights, gets a massage and then gets fully dressed for the game. He usually doesn't say a word the whole time.

Ray Allen always comes to the gym super early, gets on the treadmill, runs, and then goes on the court to get his shots up. Then he comes back to the locker room, sits down, eats a banana and reads or plays music on his iPad. He's always looking smooth, of course.

Rondo will come in and talk about cars or music or fashion or whatever he's been reading about. He has a ton of hobbies and he likes to get loose talking about them. Once he has changed into his workout clothes, he puts his iPod underneath his shirt and goes to the court to shoot free throws and jumpers. Then he goes and watches film on whoever we're playing that night. He's got a breakdown of the man who will be guarding him, and he studies every little thing over and over until it's time to go out for warm-ups.

Paul Pierce was definitely the most loose, as he should be. Boston was his city and the Celtics were his team. He was there through some tough times for the franchise and he stuck with them and won a Finals MVP and became a future hall-of-famer for them. He would come in and joke around a little bit with everybody until it was time to go out and shoot, which for him was right after Ray.

After he got his shots up he would walk around the locker room and be real vocal about what we had to do that night and about the destiny of our team. He would get us all focused and then go watch some film.

I was taking a little bit of the pregame routines from everybody. At first I would shoot with Ray, then I'd go watch film with Rondo, then I'd go and either lift or stretch with KG, then I'd go out and shoot again with Paul or whoever was out there.

When it got close to game time Doc would call us in to watch more film and break down the plays we were going to run that night. We'd go through our first three offensive sets and go down the list of how we were going to defend each guy on the other team. Then we'd get about three minutes to relax before we took the court.

It was during this time that I solved one of the biggest mysteries in the NBA: Why KG is so sweaty before the game even starts.

When I was with the Knicks and we'd play the Celtics I would always look at KG during the starting lineups and wonder why he was already dripping with sweat when the game hadn't even started yet. I know lots of fans would watch the games and think the same thing. The answer is simple.

Just before starting lineups, KG would go to the steam room in full uniform and jump around and scream and get himself loose and fired up. It was crazy. I'd pile in there with him and Rondo and Big Baby and we'd just yell our heads off and jump up and down to get the blood flowing and the adrenaline going.

I have taken each of those things from those guys and brought them to every team I've played on since.

★★★

When the postseason came around the intensity picked up throughout the organization. You could feel that this team was on a mission. Every time the Big Three talked it was about how we had one destination: the NBA Finals. Nothing else mattered. Doc talked about how we were going to all stick together for every game and how we'd be a family throughout the playoffs. It didn't matter what the media or referees or other teams said or did, it was us against the world and nobody could beat us if we hung tight.

When I heard that stuff I was all in. I wanted a ring so bad I didn't care how we got it. In the first round of that year's playoffs we played the Miami Heat, but that was before LeBron and Bosh joined Dwyane Wade and we beat them quickly in five games.

Then we fell behind LeBron's Cavs in the next series two games to one. The next night Rondo had one of the most amazing games I have ever seen. He was playing on a level that we all couldn't believe. Here you have LeBron James, Paul Pierce, Kevin

Garnett and Ray Allen on the floor and Rondo was the best player that night by far, putting up a ridiculous triple-double with 29 points, 18 rebounds and 13 assists.

That was an all-time performance and the Cavs never recovered. We blew them out the next game with Ray hitting a bunch of threes, and then in Game 6 everyone played great. I wasn't playing much during this time because of certain match-ups but I learned so much about how to prepare and stay focused during the playoffs. It was such a valuable experience for me and I knew eventually my time was going to come.

We got up quickly 3-0 on Orlando in the Eastern Conference Finals. The only tight game up to that point was Game 2 when Pierce had to hit a few late clutch free throws to ice it. I didn't play at all in the first two games and I only played a few minutes in the fourth and fifth games, which we lost.

At the beginning of the second quarter in Game 6, Rondo was hit hard and had to go to the sideline and my number was called. We had done so much preparation that I wasn't nervous at all. I knew I had to go in and do my thing until Rondo was ready to come back. I knew Doc was counting on me and I ended up scoring thirteen points in that quarter, lighting up the Magic at home.

The Boston crowd was insane that game. I could feel their energy with every shot I hit. They wanted us to get back to the Finals so bad and we were able to do that. We crushed Orlando that night and we had the Lakers up next. Finally, I was in the Finals!

★★★

Being in the NBA Finals was a dream come true, and being a part of it as a member of the Celtics, especially with Rondo and Ray and Paul and KG, made it that much sweeter. The icing on the cake was that we were going to play Kobe and the Lakers. These were probably the two most important franchises in the NBA.

We split the first two games, with Ray having a huge Game 2. It was in that game that I got my first minutes in the Finals. I tried to keep my cool and scored seven points in seven minutes. We won, and I felt good because I knew I contributed what I could in the short time I was on the floor.

Then we lost Game 3, which put is in a tough spot. We really didn't want to lose the next one and go down 3-1.

The first three quarters of Game 4 were not going well for us. We were down 62-60 and Doc decided to start the fourth quarter with Ray Allen, me, Big Baby, Rasheed Wallace and Tony Allen. At first we thought it was just a gimmick to start the quarter, but then we started taking it to the Lakers. It was one of the best quarters I've ever been involved in.

I could tell that the team was a little sluggish, so when I got in I stepped it up on defense real quick. I stole the ball from Jordan Farmar and then dove for it while calling a timeout. When we got it, I screamed and showed the ball to the fans, trying to get them fired up. They felt my passion and went berserk.

Big Baby made a few shots and got on a roll, then I got hot and we started feeding off of each other. I think he hit three layups in a row and he was yelling and shouting and drooling as the fans responded to each bucket. Somewhere in there a photographer took the famous photo of him thundering down the court while I jumped on his back. It was basketball perfection for me. There was so much energy and emotion—and this was the NBA Finals! Me and Baby were taking it to the Lakers!

Tony Allen and 'Sheed had some nice plays in there as well, so it wasn't all us, but that game is mostly remembered for how Baby and I played and how Doc kept KG, Pierce and Rondo on the bench almost the whole fourth quarter.

We outscored the Lakers by ten while we were in there. I had a dozen points and Baby had 18. During the timeouts I would look at him and say, "This is our time. Let's just go hoop like it's open gym and we're balling like we've done our whole lives. We're not in here to run plays right now. Let's ride this energy and show the world how we can play."

We won the game by seven and Baby and I were requested for the postgame press conference. That was when I made the comment about how he was like Shrek and I was like Donkey. That got a lot of traction because it fit. People could tell that we had really become good friends and those characters fit our personalities. That night was one of the best nights ever.

After that, we won Game 5 and I could taste a title. We were right there, with two chances to beat the Lakers to win the whole thing, but we ran out of steam. We got slaughtered in Game 6. Absolutely crushed. Nobody played well at all. But we still had Game 7.

Before the last game Doc told us he was going to shorten the roster a bit and go with the veterans. He played Baby a lot but Tony Allen and I barely played. There were times during that game where I thought we could have provided an energy boost, like we did during the regular season and at other spots in the playoffs, but Doc had made up his mind.

The truth is, Kobe had a bad game and Pau Gasol didn't play great and we should have won. We were ahead in the fourth quarter and then everyone went cold and flat. It was a gut-wrenching loss. Losing a Game 7 in the Finals was like nothing I had ever experienced. I was sick. It really felt like I had an illness for a while—to be that close to a title and have it slip away.

There was so much heartache in the locker room afterward. Everyone was sick to their stomachs. Then Pierce and Garnett started going around to everyone and telling us that we'd be back next year and that we'd be stronger for going through this kind of loss. It was amazing to see.

KG was telling us how much he loved us and how he'd go to war with each of us any day of the week. He said he knew there were things that we could have done differently or plays that could have gone a different way, but that's just not how it worked out.

Doc eventually talked to all of us and took a bunch of the blame. He said he didn't stick to his original game plan and that was on him. He blamed himself for some of his decisions. Then Paul and KG and Ray spoke up and wouldn't let him do that. They said they were the ones on the floor and that they had to make the shots and make the plays. There was a lot of love and respect in that room, and when it was all over, everyone was excited for next year and what the possibilities would bring.

★★★

I worked harder that summer than I ever had in my life. Doc told me all the things he wanted me to focus on—and being five minutes away from a title was all the motivation I needed. I flew back and forth from Seattle to Boston all summer to get my work in, and it paid off. Rondo was hurt early in the season and I was able to step in for him and contribute. We were scorching hot, winning 24 of our first 30 games.

When February rolled around, I started playing a lot of minutes even though my knee was bothering me and I felt like something else was up. Turns out I was right because I started hearing that Danny Ainge wanted to switch things up and that I was being shopped as trade bait. Hearing that news made me pretty upset. I told my agent there was no way I was going back to a noncontender. After all that losing with the Knicks, and then to come within five minutes of a title, and now being on one of the best teams in the NBA with great players, I had no interest in going back to a crappy team. I felt like I worked too hard for that. In the end, it's a business and we have no control over this stuff, but that's how I was feeling.

Then I found out I was traded to a team as a throw-in, and it hurt.

CHAPTER NINE

RUNNING WITH THE YOUNG GUNS IN OKLAHOMA CITY

We were in Oakland playing Golden State when I found out I was traded to Oklahoma City. I didn't get a chance to clear out my locker or my apartment or anything in Boston. Everything in my locker was packed up and shipped to my place in Seattle, and I couldn't go back to my apartment in Massachusetts until the summer. And not only was I changing teams but I had to pay for the rest of my lease in Boston and get a new lease for a place in Oklahoma City, which was aggravating. This is one of the little annoying things that happen when a guy gets traded that most people don't think about.

When the guys found out that Kendrick Perkins and I were going to the Thunder they were upset, mainly for Perk. But I had friends on that team too. Big Baby cried because we had really become close, but I felt so bad for Perk. He would have been a Boston Celtic his whole life, and he grew up with those guys. He loved KG and Pierce and all of them. He loved the city. I know it's a business, but that doesn't mean guys don't get attached to their friends and their cities.

As for me, I felt like I was going from the top of the mountain to the bottom. This wasn't because the Thunder weren't good—they were an awesome team—but I knew they really didn't want me and I was just tossed in to the trade to make it work salary cap-wise for Perk.

The other thing was that I needed knee surgery. Once I got to Oklahoma City and I knew they weren't really planning on playing me, they agreed to let me get arthroscopic surgery on my knee and rehab it.

The trade was in February and I got the surgery almost immediately. I felt really alone when I had that surgery, and the surgeon let me and my mom stay at his house for the first five days or so while I started my recovery. It was a really down time for me because I felt like I was so close to making my mark in Boston, and now I was there in OKC, having surgery for the first time to try to get healthy for a team that had a bunch of guards on the depth chart ahead of me.

I watched a ton of movies during rehab, and I used this machine that would rotate my knee and provide motion even while I slept to speed recovery. I learned to sleep with my knee moving and I know it helped me rehab faster than expected.

Still, for a long time I couldn't do many normal things. I couldn't sit or bend my leg very well. I also couldn't put on my pants or my shoes or anything that involved bringing my knee closer to me. I had a lot of time to think about where I was in my career and in my life. I had no idea what the future held but I was determined to come back stronger. I knew so many guys who had knee surgery and let the surgery get in their heads.

My doctor explained that with my surgery, I was actually getting rid of a problem so my knee would be stronger than before I went under the knife. I held on to that, keeping the rest of my body in top shape while I couldn't use my legs.

I worked out on this bike that had pedals only for your arms, and my arms got so cut. I would also bring a chair to the basketball court and sit and shoot all day. I'd make a hundred shots from one spot then pick another spot and make a hundred more. I couldn't walk but I got my shots up like I always had. I was not going to give myself any excuses. I didn't want to come back and then have to rehab my upper body.

Slowly but surely I started to move a little bit and put a little pressure on my knee. Then I could bend it and ride a bike. Eventually, I started walking again, just maybe ten feet at a time. We slowly increased distances until I could walk normally and then jog normally and then run normally. After I could run straight ahead without pain, we worked on cutting and slashing, and at around the six-week mark I was back to doing most of what I could do before—I just had to get my conditioning back.

★★★

While all of this was going on I got to know the guys in Oklahoma City pretty well. Kevin Durant and James Harden and Russell Westbrook were really cool guys. You could tell they were truly friends off the court. My apartment was right next to Perk's place, so we would hang out all the time and have our meals together when we were home. KD and Russell would come over to my house to play cards and watch other college or NBA games on off nights. I got along with those guys really well and it was fun to watch them play. I don't think people realized yet how truly great KD and Russell were.

Off the court the rehab went well and I was really getting along with my new teammates, but when I was ready to play full speed again, there wasn't room for me on the roster.

The first scrimmage I played in when I came back was in Denver. The thin air combined with how long it had been since I played made it harder than usual. The one thing I told myself was that I was going to come back 100% and that I wasn't going to take it easy. That day I came in and just dogged Russell Westbrook. I was on him all practice and we kept taking it to each other. He's so competitive and he got so mad.

"I'm showing you, Russ," I said. "Knee injury or not, I'm back and I'm gonna show what I can do. I'm pushing for playing time."

He ate it up and tried to stop me, and we had a great scrimmage.

The problem was that scrimmages were all I had. I felt like I was in basketball prison again, like I was back in New York under D'Antoni. Since it was the same situation as with the Knicks, I treated it the same way and turned my practices into my games and worked on my conditioning and skills any way that I could.

It was around this time that I got close with Royal Ivey. Royal went to the University of Texas and then was drafted in 2004 by Atlanta. He wasn't getting a lot of minutes on the Thunder either so I came up with a plan for both of us to get our work in.

Every day we got to the practice facility super early to go through our lifting and basketball workouts. Then we'd eat breakfast. After breakfast we'd get on stationary bikes and watch all the NBA highlights from the night before. We'd ride the bike right until practice started. At first it was just four or five miles. As we built our stamina, we'd end up getting in about twelve miles before practice.

On game days or other days where we didn't scrimmage on the floor, he and I would play the hardest games of one-on-one you could imagine. They were dog fights. We both had a ton of confidence and we used it as an outlet since we weren't playing in too many games. The idea was that we'd make each other better by giving each other our best shot.

We did this every day until some of the other guys who really weren't playing much wanted to get in on it. The games expanded at first to two-on-two and then four-on-four, until finally we'd get a full five-on-five going. We'd do it even on game days. We tried to simulate the intensity of a real game so that we'd be ready if our numbers were ever called.

Coach Brooks had his starting five and his set rotation, so he didn't really pay too much attention to our games. I heard he was happy that we took it upon ourselves to work hard and stay in the best shape in case we were called upon.

I called my team the Last Five, because we were the last five guys on the bench. It was a joke but it was a way to stay positive. I used to always run my mouth, reminding the guys that we were doing this because none of us were happy with where we were in our careers.

"We're not settling for this," I'd say. "I'm not happy being one of the last five guys on this team and you shouldn't be either. I could be starting in this league. I know that. Some of you could too. You think other guys in our position are working this hard? We're gonna work hard and earn minutes."

The trouble was that these games were really the only ones we'd get to play. Even in practice when we'd scrimmage, it was hard for us to get time because none of the regular starters ever wanted to come out. Coach Brooks told us to sub in when we were ready, but if Russell or one of the other guys didn't want to come out, there was nothing I could do. I just felt like I could bring so much to that team, but I was unwanted.

After a while, I stopped trying to catch Coach Brooks' eye and I focused on doing every drill and every single thing I could to be ready for the time that he'd play me. That time never really came.

The Thunder ended up going all the way to the Western Conference Finals that year. They lost to the Mavericks in five games.

Shortly after that, I had my exit interviews with Coach Brooks and the other guys at Oklahoma City and I decided I should be honest with them about what I was thinking.

"Coach, I never asked to be traded to Oklahoma City," I said. "I can tell you guys probably didn't want me here in the first place, but I was thrown in to make the deal for Perkins work. You don't owe me anything. I understand that and I respect that and I thank you for the opportunity to be on your team. You have a great group of guys here and if you keep me, I'm going to work as hard as I can to contribute. I don't care about starting, I just want an equal opportunity to earn playing time because I know what kind of player I can be and I know what I'm worth. If you're not going to play me, you don't have to sugar coat it. Just tell me and I'll respect that."

Coach Brooks and GM Sam Presti both said they understood where I was coming from and they promised to be straight with me. Later on that offseason they let me know that they didn't want me back.

CHAPTER TEN

A GOLDEN STATE OF MIND

The 2011 NBA lockout was frustrating for me because once Oklahoma City told me they didn't want me back I was a man without a team. Normally, I wouldn't worry about being a free agent, but I was afraid that with everybody focused on the lockout I wouldn't have a team when the season started.

Since I wasn't on a team and I had no place to go because of the lockout, I played ball twice a day at the 24 Hour Fitness down the street from my house. I would go for a few hours in the morning, spend time with my kids in the afternoon, then go back really late at night when nobody was there so I could work on my game. I'd go at about 11 p.m. or midnight and stay until two in the morning.

When the lockout finally ended, I was in awesome shape but I had no team to play on. It was the unhappiest I could possibly be because, for the first time in my professional life, I was watching guys play basketball on TV at the highest level and I was sitting on my couch.

"I can't wait to get out there," I'd tell my agent. "Something needs to happen soon."

My mind began to go through all these crazy scenarios. I thought maybe the Thunder or another team was bad-mouthing me to other teams. Then I thought maybe I said something I don't remember that pissed everybody off. I even started thinking about going to play in Europe or somewhere. The more time I spent on my couch watching the NBA, the more upset I got. Plus, everywhere I went around Seattle people were asking me the same things.

"Nate, how are you not on a team?"

"What's up with the NBA, Nate? Why aren't you playing?"

"Are you retiring, Nate?"

There was so much negativity that I almost couldn't take it. All I could do was work hard, thank God for my health and for my blessings, and know that I'd get another shot soon.

Finally, my agent called me while I was at home and said, "Mark Jackson is going to call you soon."

Mark Jackson was the coach of the Golden State Warriors. One of their best players, Steph Curry, had twisted his ankle and Coach Jackson thought I could help until Curry could play.

"We need some firepower, Nate," he said. "I think you can help us."

Coach Jackson and I knew each other from his days as an NBA analyst. He would always talk to me when he did our games.

"I just love the way you play," he told me once. "You play hard. You play with passion. You're one of the guys who would have done well in the '80s and '90s. You would have been a great player then and you can be a great player now."

He always talked to me like that and I really appreciated it. To have a guy like him, with his background as both a player and commentator, take an interest in getting to know me felt great.

When he called me about playing for him, we had that connection already and I was extremely grateful. I thanked him every single day.

"Coach, thank you for taking a chance on me," I told him. "Nobody believed in me and you gave me a chance. You believed that I could be something special. I'll help you guys any way that I can."

I also loved that, like me, Coach Jackson was a bit of a showman when he played. He used to do this shimmy if he made a three-pointer or had a nice pass. That attitude showed up in how he coached because he loved to have a good time and to see guys smiling.

Some games he would say to us, "I just want you guys to go out there and have fun. No rules, no plays. Just hoop."

One of the coolest things he did was before a game when he showed a short highlight tape of every player. Each guy's segment had a highlight from high school, a highlight from college and a highlight from the pros. It got everybody fired up and reminded all of us how hard we had worked to get into the NBA. We all played awesome that night.

I think I had a strong year for the Warriors. I averaged over 11 points and 5 assists a night on twenty minutes of playing time. We didn't win a lot of games and we didn't make the playoffs, but I felt good about my contributions to the team.

When the season was over I sat down with Coach Jackson and he was so positive.

"Nate, you brought a great culture to our team," he said. "You did everything we asked you to do, no problem, and I appreciate it."

I thanked him for everything he taught me and for taking a chance on me and getting me back in the league.

After that meeting, I thought that I might have an offer coming from them, but it didn't come.

At this point I was a little angry and confused. I had shown that no matter what team I was on that if I got a decent amount of minutes I could produce: I could score, I could give assists, I could get steals. I know what I can give a team. But once again, no offers were coming.

I would look at myself in the mirror and think, *You've done everything they've asked of you, Nate. All these other guys are signing big contracts and here you are, without a team. You never get the respect you deserve. This sucks.*

I couldn't help but think like that because I knew that I was in the prime of my career yet nobody wanted me on their team. I know I had a reputation when I was younger of being a hot head or of being tough to coach, but I thought I had shown with Doc and with Coach Jackson that I could fit in anywhere and make a positive difference.

That offseason I started weighing my options outside of basketball because I didn't know if I'd get another shot. Then I got a call from the Chicago Bulls and they wanted to sign me to a one-year deal. I honestly believed I was worth so much more, but I took the deal as a blessing and looked at it like I had one more year to prove that I belonged in the NBA.

CHAPTER ELEVEN

WINNING OVER THE WINDY CITY

I loved Chicago and I loved my team that year. I loved the players and the fans—and for the first time in my life I played in all 82 games of an NBA season. I even started 23 of them. I can't fully explain how rewarding that felt after everything I had been through in my career. I knew Coach Thibodeau a little from when he was an assistant coach on the Celtics. He is a hard-nosed guy, and when that type of personality meets an energy guy like me and we're on the same page, beautiful things can happen—and they did.

The greatest thing about Coach Thibodeau is how much he wants to win. He doesn't care about anything other than how you can help him be victorious. That's it. Play hard, help the team get Ws. If you can do that, you and Coach Thibodeau can get along.

I know there were probably days when he wanted to pull his hair out because of something I did on the court, but I think I minimized those times with him. The rest of the time he respected how hard I worked on playing my game in his controlled setting. Also, I know he respected my constant effort. From the first day of practice I told him, "Coach, nobody is going to work harder for you than me. I will come in every single day and practice as hard as I can. I don't care about starting or minutes. I will do whatever you need me to do. All you need to know is that I'll be ready whenever you call my number. You'll never have to worry about me being ready. Now, I know some games I might not play well, but I'll always go hard, I'll always give you energy, and I'll give you everything I have."

He responded to me with playing time. Of course, much of it was due to injuries, but he trusted me more than almost any other coach and I believe I produced for him.

Over the course of the season I averaged 13 points, 4 assists, 2 rebounds and a steal in about 25 minutes per game.

The biggest adjustment for me was getting used to starting again. When you come off the bench, you have to try to get involved right away because you know your minutes are limited. As a starter, you get a lot of chances to get going so you don't have to rush them.

My plan for when I came off the bench was to let the game come to me, but to mix things up on offense. I usually would get in the game right around the end of the first quarter and then come out with six or eight minutes left in the second quarter. That could mean anywhere from five to fifteen minutes of playing time. Most of the time it was around eight minutes, so in that eight minutes I would try to make a two-point jump shot, a layup and get to the line for some free throws. If I had an open look at a three, I'd take that also.

When I became a regular starter, I changed my entire mindset. In the first quarter my goal was to get everyone involved while I spread out my jumper, layup, three-pointer and foul shot over the first half. Once I hit each of those marks I would play freely because I'd gotten several looks at the basket from all over the floor, I knew how the defense was going to try to stop me from every spot, and I could adjust my game to succeed. It was like I set up a game within a game.

In February of 2013, Kirk Hinrich, our starting point guard with Derrick Rose out, hurt his elbow and I had to fill in as the starter.

Coach Thibodeau believed in me and I wanted to reward him with the best play of my career. At that point it felt like everything clicked for me. I averaged 17.8 points, 6.8 assists, 2.5 steals per game during that first week and, most important, we went 3-1.

For the first time in my career I was named Eastern Conference Player of the Week.

That was such a high point for me because usually guys like LeBron James or Carmelo Anthony win that honor, but here I was, barely four months from not even having a contract, being told I was too short or too streaky or too whatever to play in the NBA, and I showed the league that I can lead a team and ball with the best of them. It was a triumphant feeling.

The key for me after that was to maintain my steady play as we headed into the playoffs.

★★★

Our first-round series was against the Brooklyn Nets, who were a higher seed than us. We lost the first game in Brooklyn. Carlos Boozer had a pretty strong game and Jimmy Butler played really well, but we were a little off as a team. Personally, I was feeling it from the floor and had 17 points, but Deron Williams played great and Brooke Lopez had a good game for them inside.

Even though we lost, I was really proud of Jimmy Butler. Earlier in the year, when the injuries started piling up, I pulled Jimmy aside and told him what our responsibilities were going to be for the season. I did this not only because I wanted to win but because I was getting a first-hand look at Jimmy's game and I saw his potential.

"Jimmy, now is the time for you to show everybody that you can be a superstar," I told him. "We need you to be a star now. You have the ability to play like LeBron. I see you every day in practice and I see your moves and your ability. You're getting better every day. You need to believe in yourself and carry yourself with confidence."

After that talk Jimmy and I played one-on-one as hard as we could almost every day. I'd call him out on dogging it and he'd take it to me strong. The whole time I was telling him how great he could be. Over the course of the season, he started getting better and putting up more complete games and I'd say, "See, I told you. Show the world what you can do."

When he started performing at a high level in the playoffs I felt like a proud older brother.

Game 2 against Brooklyn was all about the third quarter, when we held the Nets to 11 points. Deron Williams made only one shot the whole game and we were able to hang on for the win on the road.

We won Game 3 and then we played the epic, three-overtime Game 4.

I will never forget that game for the rest of my life—and I'm lucky I'll remember it because I got demolished on a screen by Gerald Wallace with about seven minutes to play. That happened when I was running down the court, watching my guy and Wallace planted himself in front of me and I ran into him like he was a steel door. Boom! He completely laid me out. People said that it almost looked like a cartoon, where a character runs into a wall and just goes *splat*.

As for me, I didn't know what happened. I just knew that I got my bell rung and that it was the playoffs and that it was going to take more than a Gerald Wallace brick wall to stop me. Instead of getting mad, I decided to start getting buckets.

We were down, at home, in the playoffs, by fourteen points with under three minutes remaining. I looked at the scoreboard with about 2:55 left and I thought to myself, *We can win this game. We just need to make a few shots.*

I was also thinking that I was playing well, and if I could just catch fire for a few minutes maybe I could make some magic happen. It started when I hit a nice pull-up jumper at the foul line. That cut the lead to a dozen and the crowd got into it a little bit.

The Nets missed their next shot, and when I came down the court I could tell that I had my juices flowing and it was my time to make my move. Deron Williams was all over me but I put the ball between my legs after a nice pick from Joakim Noah and got some space for a three-pointer. Deron fouled me, so I missed the shot, but I sank all three free throws.

Those free throws cut the lead to nine and the Chicago fans were on their feet, losing it. You could feel the momentum shift in the air. It was like you could touch it or taste it. Every time we got the ball on our side of the court the roar of the crowd was deafening. I took all their sound and all their electricity and channeled it into my body. I wanted so bad to do something amazing for the city of Chicago—and the shots kept falling.

Once we had the lead down to four I felt like I wasn't going to miss again. Next time down the floor I brought the ball to the right side, slid off a screen from Joakim and as I got closer to the hoop, seven-footer Brooke Lopez closed on me so I pulled up and hit a jumper right over him. When the ball dropped in to cut the lead to two, the fans exploded. I hit the deck on the shot to avoid contact and when I got up it was like I could feel the place vibrating.

The Nets got the ball back but I was all over the inbounds pass and they were called for five seconds. Coach Thibodeau loves those kinds of plays more than anything, and even he got fired up for that one.

That gave us the ball with about a minute left. I knew the entire place was expecting me to shoot, which is why I had to switch it up. I came off a pick and roll like I had the play before, but just as the defense was collapsing on me, I dumped the ball underneath to Boozer, who hit a tough lay-up to tie the game.

Brooklyn got two points on their next possession, and then Joakim had an amazing put-back on our end to tie the game back up with about ten seconds left. Deron missed his shot at the buzzer and we went to overtime.

It was after that game was over that I was told that I scored 23 points in the fourth quarter, almost tying Michael Jordan's record of 24 points. Having my name mentioned in the same breath as Michael Jordan was one of the most unbelievable moments in my career. When I was a kid I used to want Michael Jordan to adopt me, and here I was, almost tying his record in his building. But my work wasn't done.

Once the game went into overtime, I did my best to control my energy because my meter was off the charts. We traded baskets for a bit and then things got tight again with about a minute left in the first overtime.

I felt like it was my time again and I took the ball up the court, dribbled around a screen and hit a jumper right at the tip of the horn on the Bulls logo. That put us up two, but then the Nets scored again.

On the next possession, I dumped the ball to Joakim, who found Boozer to tie the game again! It was just back and forth the whole overtime. Joe Johnson got dialed in and came down the floor and knocked down a clutch shot in traffic to put them up by two.

With the game tied and seven seconds left, I had the ball in an isolation set and knew that I was going to create something. I had Deron one-on-one and took him left and went up for a floater just past the three-point line. I have always believed that I can make any shot, and that was one of the toughest of my career. It was about an 18-foot leaning floater that went in off the backboard and gave us a two-point lead with only a few seconds left.

I thought we had the game locked up, but once again, Joe Johnson hit a tremendous shot to tie the game and we went to a second overtime.

At the end of the second overtime, I was dribbling the ball and Deron Williams flopped when I leaned into him. They called an offensive foul on me and I couldn't believe it. In the middle of that kind of game to make that kind of call was unbelievable. But it happened and I fouled out.

At that point it was up to my boys to take it home, and they did. The game went into a third overtime and every guy chipped in to get that win.

We were ecstatic after that game. I remember the press conference, and when someone asked Boozer how we got back into the game after being down by so much, he said, "We got a stop and gave the ball to Nate. Then we got a stop and gave the ball to Nate. Then we got a stop and gave the ball to Nate."

I just laughed. I ended up scoring 34 that game, and there's nothing cooler than to hear people refer to that game as "The Nate Robinson Game."

★★★

I started the next game because Hinrich was hurt and I played almost 45 minutes. At that point we had so many injuries it was almost a joke. Hinrich was out, Derrick Rose was still out and Luol Deng had the flu.

On top of all that, I was extremely sick during the game and was throwing up in garbage cans during timeouts. It was hard gutting it out with that kind of stomach bug, but I knew we had nobody else and it was my job to be as tough as I could and play as hard as I could. My motto was "just puke and get back out there."

At halftime, they gave me fluids and electrolytes. None of it mattered. Whatever I drank I just threw up again. The entire halftime I'd drink something and vomit in a bucket. Then when I got back on the floor, I felt like I had to vomit the whole time. At one point, I didn't want to go on the floor, so I just fouled my guy and ran off to puke. When I was done, I went back out.

After the game some reporters tried to make something of the fact that I was playing through a horrible stomach virus while Derrick Rose was fully practicing but not playing in any games.

"Don't do that, guys," I said. "I've had a knee injury before and you can't come back until you're ready. There's nothing worse than coming back and getting reinjured. Derrick will come back when he's ready and he'll come back stronger."

I truly believed that. I even talked to him about it a bunch and told him, "It's your life and your career. Don't let anyone tell you when you should come back. You'll know and when you do you'll kill it."

After losing that game and Game 6, we had to go on the road for Game 7.

★★★

Heading into Game 7 in Brooklyn I was thinking about my Mean Machines team from back in grade school. I thought about when we were down and how everyone was crying and I got the guys fired up and ready to play. Now, here we were, all these years later going into a Game 7, on the road, with so many of our best players hurt. It felt like that same kind of situation.

"We're not ready to go home, guys!" I said in the locker room. "I've seen this before. I've dreamt this. You guys have to believe me. It's our time to shock the world. Nobody thinks we can win with all of these injuries, but we're going to win tonight. We're going to beat Brooklyn. Believe in yourselves."

Joakim, who is really big into positive energy, and Carlos and Taj Gibson and Jimmy, they all started buying into it and we went out and played a hell of a game. Especially Joakim. He had a monster night, scoring 24, getting 14 rebounds and blocking six shots. He was our emotional leader that night. We built a huge lead in the second quarter and held them off to advance.

"I told you!" I shouted to everyone. "I told you! We shocked the world!"

After the game guys were thanking me for bringing the energy and positivity and toughness that I had throughout the series. I used to write in my journal all the time, "Don't be afraid to shock the world."

And here I was, doing just that. Next up was LeBron James, Dwyane Wade, Chris Bosh and the World Champion Miami Heat. I opened this book with my thoughts on that and how that game and series went, so I won't repeat myself now.

All I can say is that I honestly thought we had a chance to win that series.

CHAPTER 12

A NEW TEAM, A NEW DREAM

I believe that year in Chicago was the most complete, best season I had in the NBA. I felt like my performance down the stretch and in the playoffs spoke for itself. When the playoffs were over there was no exit interview or anything. The Bulls organization basically said, "Go home."

I flew back to Chicago from Miami and hung out for a little while and then went home to Seattle. People were in my ear during that playoff run and afterward, talking about how much money I was making myself by playing as well as I did and how it was perfect that I was a free agent.

I've had too many ups and downs in my career to think that way. I knew deep down that's just not how my career has gone. Every year it feels like I have to prove myself over and over. My first choice would have been to get a long-term deal from the Bulls. I know they had Derrick Rose coming back, but I thought about all the possibilities of having the two of us on the floor at the same time. I think that would have posed so many problems for other teams because most teams don't have two players who can guard guys as quick as us, so it would be a pick-your-poison situation.

Guys in the media were either up on me or down on me, but the one guy who I thought had my back was Stephen A. Smith. During the playoffs and after he was telling the truth about how effective I could be and what I could do for teams. It seemed like he was the only one out there who understood my value and I have always appreciated him for it.

When the Bulls didn't make an offer for me I took it in stride. I was hurt because I felt like I gave them everything I had and I did everything Coach Thibodeau asked of me—we won a playoff series nobody thought we could win. I also loved my teammates. I got along so well with Jimmy and Carlos and Joakim and all of them. I felt like we could have done some special things together.

When I let my mind wander none of it made sense. I had a good year with Golden State, I reached a new level with the Bulls, and I felt like I deserved a long contract. I wanted a marriage-like commitment to a team, to go to a place where I would play for a long time and retire there. It just wasn't in the cards that offseason.

While I was looking at offers from teams I signed with the Jordan Brand, which was always a dream of mine. I also joined the Pepsi Max ad campaign with Kyrie Irving, where we dress up as retired old guys and go to basketball courts and hustle young guys. I'm sure you've seen the ads. My character is Uncle Lights. It's awesome and it was something I always wanted to do. We started the State of Nate website and reality show about my life. I design and sell shirts and eventually I want to do sneakers too.

I have huge plans for when my playing career is over. I want to open a big athletic facility in Seattle to host basketball tournaments and camps. I'd like to use it to run programs for kids as a way to give back to the community I love so much.

But I have a lot of years of basketball left in me. My new contract with the Denver Nuggets is a multi-year deal, which is what I wanted. I hope it gives me the platform to show the city what I can do, and maybe it'll lead to success in the playoffs and another contract.

I don't know what the world holds for me or what God's plan is for me. I just know that I give 100% to my family, 100% to basketball and I'm extremely blessed for everything that I have.

PART II

ON DUNKING

CHAPTER THIRTEEN

BORN TO JUMP

Most babies sit, then crawl, then walk, then run, and somewhere after that, they learn how to jump. I was a little different. I was jumping first. My mother says that before I was really crawling and before I could stand on my own she would hold both of my hands and I could jump in the air. I know most babies will bounce up and down to strengthen their legs if you hold them up, but my mom and other members in my family swear that I actually had hops as a baby. At six months old I was getting air practically before I could roll over.

As far back as I can remember I was obsessed with jumping and touching stuff that was too high for other kids to touch. Before I even played sports, if I saw a counter or a door frame or just a picture or mark on the wall, I instinctively leapt for it. If there were any adults around, they would usually look at me like I was an alien or something because here I was, this little kid, getting a foot or two off the ground.

Once I was old enough to understand sports, my dad showed me videos of all the NBA dunk contests. The one dunk I remember most, which is the one many people remember most, is Michael Jordan's dunk from the foul line.

"You like that, son?" my dad would ask. "You want to have your pilot's license like Air Jordan?"

After he saw me taking an interest in Jordan, he showed me tapes of Dominique and Dr. J and I was in awe. I couldn't believe how high and how far those guys could jump. Plus, they had long arms and long legs, which made the dunks look artistic. I never knew I was going to top out at 5'9", but I knew I wasn't going to be 6'6" either.

The first time I saw video of Spud Webb dunking I thought, *OK, this guy is showing me what's possible. I don't have to be 6'5" or taller to succeed.*

Right around this time Allen Iverson was lighting up the Big East with Georgetown, and he became my motivation. He was fearless and he was so small. I know he was listed at 6', but he looked shorter than that. And he looked like he weighed about 150 pounds. None of that mattered. He straight up dominated everyone. I wanted to look like him and be him. He's why I started getting tattoos.

I could dunk a volleyball in middle school. I dunked my first basketball in eighth grade. My entire high school team could dunk, so that wasn't a big deal for my town because they were used to seeing it. When we'd go on the road, especially once I got stronger and could really throw down as a sophomore and later as a senior, I would rip some serious dunks in warm-ups to intimidate the other team. Most people have never seen someone my size crush dunks like that in person. I loved seeing the looks on their faces.

What most people don't realize is that if I actually had big hands, I could do much more on a dunk. I can't palm a ball, so I have to cuff it and get at least three inches more above the rim than I would have to if I could just hold the ball in one hand. If I grab a kid's ball or a volleyball I can do some nasty, nasty dunks.

Once I made it to the NBA, I wanted to be in the dunk contest like Spud Webb. When I told my agents and they asked the league about it, they told me that I had to start getting dunks in games so they could see what I could do.

I knew there was a lot of footage out there of my dunks from college and practices and other stuff, but if they wanted to see me dunk in NBA games, then so be it.

One of my first major dunks in the NBA was on James Posey when we played the Heat. The dunk was extra special because one of my childhood idols from Seattle, Gary Payton, was right there on the play. He was in the paint when I threw it down, and that night it was like the league took notice. I made all the highlight shows and it was all over the internet.

After that I tried to dunk on everyone. I tried to dunk on Dwyane Wade. I tried to dunk on LeBron. I tried to dunk on Shaq. Every time I'd get on a fast break or get in the lane and had a path to dunk, I would go for it. The way I saw it, if I dunked on someone I'm a hero because I'm short, and if they block me or stuff me, they're supposed to because they're so much bigger. It was a win-win situation for me—but I never, ever want to get blocked.

The more I dunked the more the buzz grew about me being in the 2006 dunk contest. Finally, a little while before the All-Star break I got the call that I was in—it was my chance to make history.

★★★

Right after it was announced that I was in, I got a text from Jamal Crawford. The text said, "Call me."

Jamal and I are close, but he never talks on the phone, so I knew he had something to tell me.

"Must be big news if you want me to call you, Jamal," I said.

"Bro, I have the perfect idea for you in the dunk contest," he said. "You should jump over Spud Webb. It's been twenty years since he won. You bring back a dunking icon, who's about 50 years old now, and you jump over him to pay homage to him. You nail that dunk, you change the history of the dunk contest and you win. Trust me."

"Hell yeah," I said. "That is an awesome idea. How do we get in touch with Spud?"

"I got this," he said. "Coach Herb Williams knows him really well. They're good friends. We can ask him."

The next day we talked to Coach Williams and he got in touch with Spud, who agreed to talk to me.

"I'll do it," Spud said. "But, I have one question."

"What?" I asked.

"Can you even jump over me?" he asked.

"No doubt," I said.

★★★

All-Star Weekend that year was in Houston and I brought my family and my friends. I wasn't there to put on a show and see what happens; I wanted to win. The day before the contest I was able to practice my dunks at the Houston Rockets' training facility. I worked out a little bit, got a sweat going, and then I got creative. I was alone for a while when all of a sudden, the legend, Spud Webb walks into the gym.

"It's a pleasure to meet you," I said. "I can't believe I'm really talking to you. I've watched all your dunks. You've been an inspiration to me for so long. You paved the way for me. When I saw how high you jumped and how tall you were, I thought to myself, *I want to jump like that.* You helped me believe I could do it."

Spud was cool. He thanked me and we talked for a bit—then we got down to business.

"I want you to bounce it so I can run up, jump over you and catch the ball in the air," I said.

"I can do that," he said.

"It has to be perfect timing," I said. "If you bounce it too early I'm going to miss the ball. Bounce it right when you see me start running toward you."

The first time we practiced he didn't even have a ball. I put him where I wanted him to stand and I made sure that I could jump over him, which I did no problem. Then I gave him the ball.

"All I'm doing is jumping as high as I can to meet the ball in the air," I said. "Once I get it the energy will flow through me to my hands and I'll throw it down."

We nailed it the first try. One take. Boom. Done. It was perfect. I texted Jamal to thank him for his vision because he saw this moment, and now I knew it was going to be possible the next night. Spud and I talked a little more and he gave me some great advice.

"Have fun, man," he said. "Enjoy it. Remember all those times when you wanted to dunk in a game to show the world what you can do, and harness that."

"I will," I said. "I'm going to do all the dunks that I try when I'm just with my friends."

"Exactly," he said. "Just think about it like you're in a gym by yourself. Don't even think about the people."

"Thanks," I said. "See you tomorrow night."

★★★

Josh Smith won the Dunk Contest in 2005 and I knew he'd be tough to beat. Hakim Warrick was also in the contest and he was a nice dunker too. The guy who most people thought would go right to the finals was Andre Iguodala. I agreed. I knew I was going to have to complete some solid slams to beat him.

I decided that the best way to win was to map out every dunk in advance and stick to it no matter what. Even if a guy did the exact same dunk right before me, I would just have to do it better. You can always tell when a guy doesn't have a plan because he takes a while before his dunks and then doesn't have much confidence for each one. Also, so much of the dunk contest is about showmanship. If you're spending time thinking about what dunk you want to do, you won't be able to get the crowd into it.

When I stepped on the floor for my first dunk I realized how different this whole experience was. All eyes are on you, and these aren't the normal eyes of just a home or away NBA crowd. This was All-Star Weekend. All the best players in the game were there and so were many legends of the game. Clyde Drexler, one of my all-time favorite dunkers, was even judging the contest.

In addition, there were a ton of celebrities in the stands and a worldwide audience. My first thought was that I wanted to represent for my family and my city. I also thought about how many dunk contests I had watched and the odds I had beaten to actually participate in one. How many kids watch the dunk contest and pretend to be in it? Tens of millions, at least. And here I was, competing. It felt great.

I got a 49 out of 50 on my first dunk. It was a 180 with a smooth bounce and the crowd went crazy. Even though I'd been in the league for a year and I had dunked a bunch of times in games, I don't think too many people realized what I was capable of until that moment.

In the second round I did a two-handed alley-oop from Quentin Richardson that I thought was a strong dunk. I don't think people understand how hard it is to get high enough to dunk with two hands, especially at my height. The crowd reacted and it got me to the final round against Iguodala.

The next dunk was the one that took me seven or eight tries. It was a really tough dunk, where I bounced the ball and brought it between my legs to dunk. I had completed it a dozen times in practice; I just didn't have the timing in the contest. After a few misses, I could hear the announcers talking about me getting tired or needing a break, but that wasn't the case. I wasn't tired. I was frustrated. I can do that dunk ten times in a row.

Finally, the crowd started cheering and I nailed it. I got a 44 on that dunk. I know it would have been much higher if I hit it the first time.

Iguodala finished a nice dunk for a fifty, and I knew it was time to bring out my trump card. I got a Spud Webb jersey and went over to find Spud in the stands. Spud smiled and the crowd ate it up and roared for him, which was cool to see. I gave him the ball and he went to the spot on the court that we practiced the day before.

Just like the day before, the timing, the jump, it was all perfect and I nailed it on the first try! I gave a nice glide motion when I hit the ground and the place went bananas. I watched the replay and I cleared Spud's head by more than when I did the practice jump.

Iguodala got a 46 on his next dunk, which put us into a tie. That meant we'd have to go to dunk contest overtime.

In overtime, I had the idea to try a dunk off the backboard from about half-court. I couldn't get a pass I liked for a while and when I did, I missed it. The crowd was chanting, "Nate! Nate! Nate! Nate!" I wanted so bad to complete that dunk that I just kept going for it. I did it on my thirteenth try. It really was a strong dunk and I was glad the crowd stuck with me on it. I got a 47. Iguodala went through his legs for a reverse and got only a 46, which meant I won.

It was one of the best moments of my career.

"It's a great honor, a great privilege to be in my shoes right now," I said in the interview afterward. "I just thank God, because without him, nothing would be possible. I also want to thank Spud for helping me out."

I've known Iguodala from when he played at Arizona and I was at Washington. We joke around whenever we see each other. He's always saying that I robbed him—and I always remind him that it was a fan vote and I can't help it if I'm more popular than he is. We always laugh about it. One time he was busting on me and I said, "You're tall and I'm short. There are more short people than tall people out there. They relate to me better."

He laughed.

★★★

The aftermath of the contest was a whirlwind of photos, media interviews, celebrity meetings and fans. In one night I became a dunking icon. It was like all of a sudden everyone in the league knew who I was. Later that night Shaq came up to talk to me.

"Dude, you're so small," he said. "I never knew you had that level of hops."

So many other players came up to me that it took hours to get back to the hotel to celebrate.

The ripple effect of that night was beyond what I could have ever imagined. When I got back to New York, Ben Stiller came up to me at a game and just looked at me.

"We're the same height!" he said. "How do you jump so high? How do you do it?"

"How do you make so many funny movies?" I asked him.

I could not believe that guys like Ben Stiller, who I loved from so many movies, were now coming up to talk to me. I gave him my shoes after that game to give to his son and he was really appreciative.

Another comedian I love is Will Ferrell, and we have actually gotten to know each other a little bit. One of my favorite movies ever is "Talladega Nights." I've probably seen it a million times. The name I used to use for road games at hotels was even Ricky Bobby. My boy Wilson Chandler would use the name Cal Naughton, and we would always do the Shake 'n Bake move from the movie. Every time I'd score and he was around I would do the Shake 'n Bake with him.

Some people picked up on it and eventually Will Ferrell made his way to a game at Madison Square Garden.

When I got to the arena that night people were telling me, "Your buddy is going to be at the game tonight."

"My buddy?" I asked.

"Will Ferrell!" they said.

"Dude, look," one of my teammates said.

Then he handed me a list of who was going to be in celebrity row and it said "Will Ferrell."

"No way!" I said. "I have to have a great game."

I was amped when I saw him in the stands but I started off a little slow. Also, I wasn't on his side of the court every time I scored. At some point one of the media guys interviewed him and he said, "I'm just waiting on my guy Nate Robinson to give me a Shake 'n Bake, but he hasn't Shake 'n Baked me yet. I'm kind of disappointed."

Finally, I hit a shot and ran over and slapped fives with him. A little later, I came off a pick and roll and rose up for a three and got fouled. The shot went in and I had a chance for a four-point play. Before I took my foul shot, I walked all the way over to Will and I gave him a full Shake 'n Bake. We got a picture of it and it's one of my favorites.

The announcer even started screaming "Shake 'n Bake!" after every basket I made. I was so energized—I scored 41 points and we beat the Pacers.

I played in an exhibition two-on-two game a little while later when he was promoting his movie "Semi-Pro." It was me and "Today" host Meredith Vieira against Will Ferrell and Woody Harrelson. That was an unbelievable experience because they had Bob Costas announcing and all these fans in the studio. The game was just for fun and it was cool to see Will again.

One of the last times I saw him I gave him one of my green Kryptonite Dunk Contest jerseys.

"Thank you for all the laughs," I told him. "You have no idea how much you've made me smile over the years. I never really met you before but you made so much of my life so happy with your movies."

He was pretty blown away and we stayed in touch after that.

When he was filming "The Other Guys" with Mark Wahlberg, he invited me to the set for a day. It was the scene where he and Wahlberg almost get blown up while they're walking away from an insurance building. I hung out with both Will and Mark and I kept thinking to myself, *Here I am, socializing with two of the biggest movie stars ever, and it's all because of the dunk contest.*

CHAPTER FOURTEEN

SLAM DUNK ICON

I lost the contest the following year to Gerald Green, who I let dunk over me for one of his dunks, and then I took the next year off, where Dwight Howard won it with the whole Superman thing.

I knew Dwight had to defend his title the next year, and it got me thinking about challenging him. One day I was watching one of his highlights and an idea hit me. I called my agent immediately.

"I want to do the dunk contest this year," I said.

"Why, you already won." he replied.

"I've got the perfect idea," I said. "You get me in the dunk contest and I'll tell you. I don't want it to leak out."

"OK," he said. "But you should tell me the idea because we'll have to plan for whatever you want to do."

"Fine," I said. "You know how Dwight Howard is Superman, right?"

"Yeah," he said.

"Well," I said. "You know what beats Superman, don't you?"

"Kryptonite," he said.

"Nope," I said. "Not kryptonite. Krypto-Nate."

"Oh my God," he said. "That is unreal. You just thought of that?"

"Yeah. Sick, right?" I said. "And I thought it all out. We already have the green Knicks jerseys from St. Patrick's Day. I'll wear one of those and have Nike make me a Kryptonite shoe and ball. I'll go all in on the kryptonite theme. The only thing I need to make sure I can do is my finale."

"What do you have in mind?" my agent asked.

"I gotta find out if Dwight Howard would be cool with me jumping over him," I said.

"Can you even jump over him?" my agent asked.

"Of course I can," I said.

When I said that, I was confident about it, but I really wasn't sure. The next day in practice I pulled aside Jared Jeffries, who is about the same size as Dwight, and I asked him if I could dunk over him.

"Just don't break my neck," he said. "Or yours."

"I won't," I said.

A bunch of guys on the team heard us talking and wanted to see if I could do it, so now I had an audience. I put Jared where I wanted him to go and I measured my distance a few times. Once I thought he was in the right place I grabbed a ball, ran up and slammed it clear over him.

"Did you just dunk that!?" he asked.

"Yup," I said. "I'm about to win myself a dunk contest."

★★★

When I got to the dunk contest the only thing that was on my mind was talking to Dwight. I knew the idea was good and that we could put on a great show, but it all hinged on him agreeing to be a part of it.

"Hey Dwight," I said, when I finally saw him. "Let me run something by you. I have a dunk that I want to do, but I'm going to need your assistance. This is going to change both our lives. We're going to be heroes forever if we do this."

I told him my idea, and then I let him know that I understood if he didn't want to do it. His first response was the same as Jared's.

"My only question is, can you jump over me?" he asked.

"Yeah, I can, trust me," I said. "You put on your Superman cape and shoes and the whole thing, and we'll put on the best show ever."

"Alright," he said. "I'm in."

"For real?" I asked, making sure.

"Yeah," he said.

And that was it. He didn't check with anybody or anything. He was so cool about it. He understood that it was a show and that it was something people would want to see. He's a guy who likes to have fun and there was no way this wasn't going to be fun.

I wasn't able to meet up with Dwight the day before because he was an All-Star, and we both had crazy schedules. That meant we didn't get to practice the dunk until the day of the event. That night, I asked him to meet me a little early on the warm-up court so we could try it once before anyone else came down there.

When we got together he asked me again if I could really jump over him.

"Let me show you," I said.

I put him at about the same spot on the floor that I put Jared when I jumped over him, I lined it up, walked back a few steps, and then ran toward him and dunked right over him.

"No way you just did that!" he said.

"Told you," I said. "You just have to wear all of your Superman gear. And just so you know, I'm going to wear a green jersey, I have some crazy green shoes from Nike and I'm going to be Krypto-Nate."

"Bro, this is crazy," he said. "You're going to be a hero."

★★★

Heading in to that weekend I thought the hardest part would be getting Dwight Howard to agree to let me jump over him. As it turned out, the hardest part happened after he said yes, when someone stole my Kryptonate shoes from my hotel room!

When I told Nike about my plans to dunk as Kryptonate the guys over there designed me a bright green shoe to go along with the theme. When I got to Phoenix they had someone deliver the shoes to my room in this sweet Kryptonate Box.

"We want you to wear them around the room to get a feel for them," the Nike rep said. "Just walk around and jump a little so you know they fit right. But don't wear them out of the room. We want people to see them for the first time at the contest."

The morning of the dunk contest I walked around my room and jogged a little and they felt great. I left to eat breakfast and do some media, and when I came back my brand-new, one-of-a-kind Kryptonate shoes were gone!

"They're not here!" I said on the phone to my agent.

"No way," he said.

"I'm telling you," I said. "They're gone. I tore my room up!"

I spent an hour going through every part of my room. Under the beds, the closet, every suitcase, every drawer and closet shelf—nothing. They were gone. I was devastated. And the thing was, nothing else was missing. It wasn't like someone broke in to take my money or jewelry or anything else valuable. My shoes were the only things missing.

It was so frustrating because the shoes were made just for me and they had a Kryptonate logo embedded in the shoe. Nobody even knew they existed except me, my agent and some people at Nike. That's what made us think someone from the inside might have stolen them.

My agent called Nike and told them what had happened, and fortunately my pair of shoes were actually two-of-a-kind. Nike made one pair and a back-up pair. I breathed one of the biggest sighs of relief ever. I don't know what I would have done if they were gone. It would have ruined the whole idea!

Later on we found out that someone either from Nike or somewhere else leaked info about my shoe, stole it and tried to auction it off or sell it back to Nike for $25,000. I have no idea how they got in my room. There was a lot of drama afterward between the guy who took them and Nike, but Nike got them back. They had to because the shoes made for me had the 'K' Kryptonate logo on them, which was different from the limited run of shoes they were going to sell that had an 'NR' logo on them.

Nike also made a neon green ball for me to match the shoes. The whole thing was unreal to me. It was like I was creating a villain, because at the time Dwight Howard was the dunk contest champion and he had the whole Superman thing going. Everyone loves Superman, so I was going to be the bad guy in a fun way to take him down.

Once the shoe issue was settled, I could relax until the contest.

★★★

The night of the contest I was feeling a little bit of pressure, because now that I had the shoes and the ball and the whole Kryptonate persona, I had to produce and get to the finals against Dwight. Also, I wasn't going to break out the green jersey, shirt and shoes until Dwight came in as Superman, so I needed him to do well too.

In the early rounds I was doing dunks that I knew I could complete and thought would give me the best shot to get to the finals. That was when Dwight dunked on a twelve-foot hoop. When I saw him do that, I realized how generous he was to let me jump over him. He worked on his dunks for the contest just as hard as I did on mine, and I think we both knew that if it came down to the end, and I jumped over him, I had a good shot of winning. I thank him every time I see him for agreeing to do it.

After that contest, people started asking me if I could dunk on a twelve-foot hoop. I can't. The highest I have ever touched is 11'8". And I only touched it. That doesn't include the ball.

Before the twelve-foot rim came out, Dwight went into a booth for the Superman transformation, with the music playing and the whole Clark Kent act going. It was awesome.

After he hit his dunk, I left and put on my green jersey and got the green ball and put on the shoes. Then I got Dwight his cape and gave it to him and told him where to stand.

I never told anyone what I was doing, but Kenny Smith and some of the other announcers immediately picked up on the kryptonite theme and even got the Kryptonate stuff. It was all part of being a showman, and the buzz in the building really picked up. Even when I was talking to Dwight and putting him in the right spot, I could hear people looking at us and saying, "How's that little dude gonna jump over Dwight Howard?"

When I walked off my steps to get ready for the dunk, people were raising their hands and getting the crowd on its feet. Even Dwight was raising his arms, telling people to stand up. Then, 3... 2... 1... We made history. I took off and I cleared him and we're both dunk contest legends. That picture of me clearing Dwight, with my legs spread and him looking up, is one of the most iconic dunk images of all time.

When you look at guys who have won memorable dunk contests, like Spud and Dominique and Michael Jordan and Vince Carter and Dwight and me, it all comes down to showmanship. People remember Dee Brown because he bent down to pump up his shoes. You have to have that classic moment that will stand out in people's minds forever. To have two dunk champions competing at the highest level and collaborating on a dunk is something that doesn't usually happen. We'll both be remembered for it.

★★★

Since I won in 2009, I was automatically invited to defend my title in 2010. I went up against Gerald Wallace, DeMar DeRozan and Shannon Brown. Some people said I shouldn't do it because I had nothing left to prove: I had jumped over Spud Webb; I jumped over Dwight Howard; I did the Kryptonate thing.

I thought that All-Star Weekend was for the fans, and if the fans wanted to see me dunk, I'd dunk.

My first dunk in the 2010 contest was an alley-oop bounce pass into a forward windmill. I got pretty high up on that one and I knew it was a decent first-round dunk. My next dunk was a 360 bounce pass that was awesome. Danilo Gallinari gave me a sweet pass and I was able to knock that one down for another trip to the finals. DeRozan had some solid dunks, but I saved my best for last: an alley-oop off the backboard into a reverse double clutch.

Spike Lee was at that contest, and once I saw his reaction I knew I won. Since we were in Dallas, I grabbed some of the pom-poms from the Cowboys cheerleaders who were at the game and I made a T.O. sign since Terrell Owens was there. He was also on Team Jordan and I thought that would be a cool tie-in. The hometown crowd loved it and I became the first three-time NBA dunk champion in history.

★★★

Over the years, family and friends and fans have suggested a lot of dunks for me to try. Some were ridiculous. Some were impossible. And some I actually did. Now that my dunk contest days are probably over, I can say that of all the people who gave me ideas, Shaq had the craziest.

One year he suggested that I spend all night of the dunk contest surrounded by little people so I would look huge, instead of looking little around NBA guys. Another time he suggested that I get carried out by a group of female bodybuilders like I was the king of Egypt or something, because, after all, I was the dunk contest king. His ideas were always out there and always hilarious.

Jamal Crawford, who gave me the idea to jump over Spud Webb, once had an idea for me to jump over the skyline of the city we were playing in. We looked around to find someone who could build that stuff but it was too complicated.

One idea that I had was to build a miniature toilet bowl to place on the rim. Then I'd dunk it and flush it at the same time. I thought that would be so funny and unique. The crowd would've loved it, I'm sure, but I never got to it.

The year the All-Star Game was in Las Vegas I wanted to dunk over a Playboy Bunny at a blackjack table. The plan was that as she flipped over a card, I'd take a card out of my shoe while I dunked and the hand would be blackjack. That would have been a major crowd pleaser. We didn't do it because the NBA didn't want to look like they were promoting gambling.

I know that no matter what I do in the NBA I will be known mostly for winning dunk contests. While I want to show the world that I can do so much more, and I think I have, I embrace that reputation. Still, I never stayed for the All-Star Game on Sunday because I only want to go to the All-Star Game when I'm selected for it.

Despite my success as a dunker and having proved people wrong by staying in the league so long, my ultimate goal is to win an NBA Championship. I would love to play on a Team USA too, but I know that probably won't happen. After winning a title, my personal goals are to be an All-Star or maybe win a Sixth Man of the Year award. When I look back on my career after it's over, I still want to be known as the baddest little dude to ever play the game, which is exactly what I told Ray Allen before I was even in the NBA.

The two ways I can make that happen are by dunking on people bigger than me and blocking people bigger than me.

My most famous block is probably the one I had on Yao Ming. That one was set up to be a classic, with the tallest guy in the league being blocked by the shortest. The block was all anticipation and remembering the fundamentals of basketball.

If your man is in the corner on the front side of the court from where you are and he dumps it off to the big man, that's your help. There's a little luck involved because you have to be in the right place at the right time to challenge the shot. When Yao got the ball I was practically in the air already. I had seen him play so much I just had a feeling he was going to go straight up with it.

I could feel the timing as I left my feet.

"I've got to win this," I said to myself. "Get up there and block it. It's David versus Goliath. Swat that ball!"

As I kept going up, Yao did exactly what I thought he would and I blocked his shot. Madison Square Garden exploded on that one!

The only thing was that I poked him in the eye after the block, so he kneeled over with his head in his hand. But that made the block look even more powerful.

That block changed some kids' lives. I got thousands of letters from them telling me that I was their hero because they were short like me and I blocked the biggest guy in the league. It made them feel like they could do anything too. It was so cool to hear from them.

I once had a big block on LeBron that was on SportsCenter a lot. I've blocked Dwight Howard and Dwyane Wade. One of my favorite blocks was on Shaq.

That block happened when he was with Cleveland and I was with New York. It was perfect because he had a huge block on me earlier in the game when I came down the lane and shot a floater and he swatted it away, putting me on my butt.

I knew I needed to get my revenge after that. When the Cavs had the ball, I was at the top of the key guarding my man when Shaq got the ball. He made a spin move and I knew he was going up with it. I ran over to help on defense and jumped before he got off the ground. Right when he was going to release it I knocked it clean out of his hand and he fell down.

"Ahhh!" I shouted. "Get that shot out of here, Kazaam!!!"

He was so mad. He started telling me that I fouled him, but I knew I didn't. Also, the ref didn't call a foul because it was clean.

I take as much pride in my blocks as I do my dunks because it shows that I can make an impact on defense, which is something I work really hard on. Because of my height, all my blocks have a legendary feel, so I don't mind being known as a giant slayer when it comes to that. I have my list of big men that I've wanted to take down, and I'm going through it one by one, on my way to proving that I can do anything the taller guys can do. After all, that's what I've been doing my whole career and that's what I'll continue to do as long as I can.

★★★

For behind-the-scenes photos of Nate's incredible life, please visit: www.stateofnate.com

★★★

ABOUT THE AUTHORS

Nate Robinson

Nate Robinson is a veteran NBA star originally from Seattle, WA, known for his explosive scoring and leaping ability. Robinson has made his mark with the New York Knicks, Boston Celtics, Chicago Bulls and Denver Nuggets. He is the NBA's first three-time slam dunk champion, despite standing only 5'9" tall.

Jon Finkel

Jon Finkel is an award-winning author and national magazine feature writer. He has been a cover story writer for *Men's Fitness*, a columnist for *GQ* and a contributor to *Men's Health*, *Details*, *ComedyCentral.com* and many more. He is currently a feature writer for Yahoo! Sports' ThePostGame.com. His previous books include *The Dadvantage* and *The Three Dollar Scholar*. His work can be seen at www.jonfinkel.com and you can follow him on Twitter at @Jon_Finkel.

Made in the USA
San Bernardino, CA
18 April 2018